THE SOUTHERN WAY

£11.00

CW00481208

CONTENTS

© Kevin Robertson (Noodle Books) and the various contributors 2011
ISBN 978-1-906419-46-2
First published in 2011 by Kevin Robertson
under the **NOODLE BOOKS** imprint
PO Box 279 Corhampton
SOUTHAMPTON
SO32 3ZX
www.noodlebooks.co.uk
editorial@thesouthernway.co.uk
Printed in England by
The Information Press

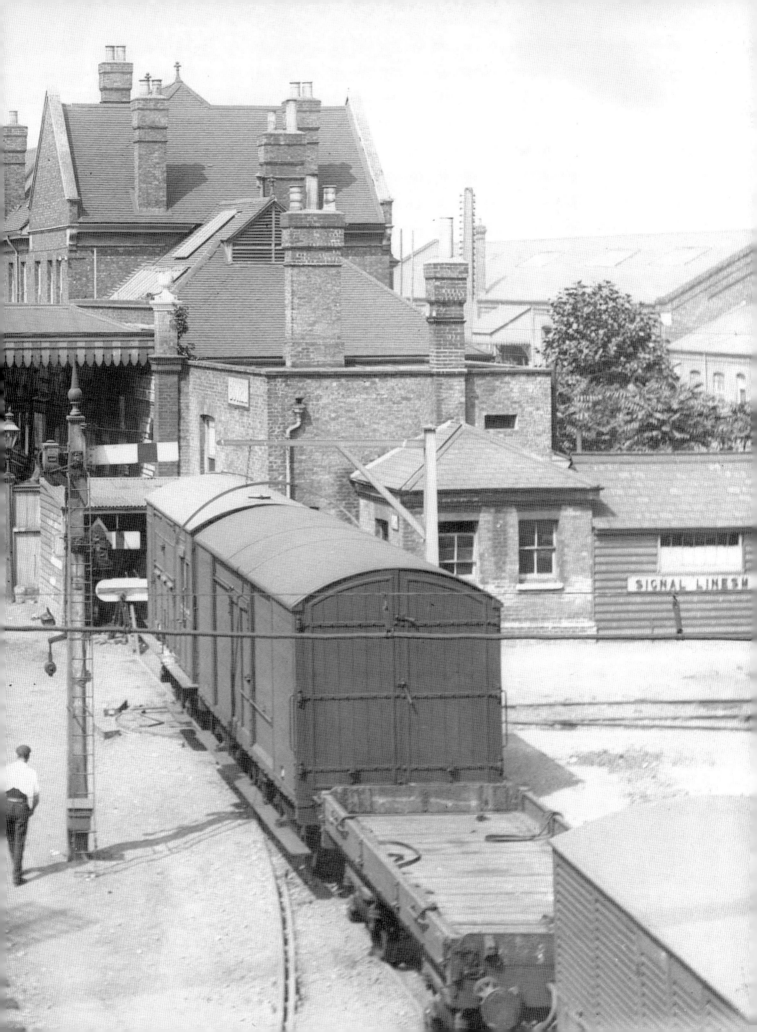

Pages 2 /3 - *Guildford in the early years of the century. The view is looking north from the Farnham Road overbridge with a Waterloo - Portsmouth service, hauled by L12 No. 412 coming to rest in the platform. As with all such wonderful panoramic scenes, there is wealth of detail which only comes out upon close examination: the signal linesman's hut, wagon turntable, engine pit, horse box, carriage truck etc. etc. Rebuilding of the station into the form seen took place in the 1880s, to remain then basically unaltered for almost a century. In the right background is the roof of the goods shed.*

This page - *Continuing the Guildford theme, two views of the station from the 19th century. In the top view the camera is looking south through the old station complete with its overall roof which spanned the two lines seen. There was a further single line out of camera to the right. In the bottom view the men are purported to be working on the rebuilding of the station. (RCHS - Spence Collection)*

Front cover - *The relative similarities (and differences) between Bulleid and BR Standard Mk 1 vehicles are contrasted in this view of rebuilt MN No. 35026 Lamport & Holt Line awaiting departure from Waterloo, probably in 1964. The BR coach may be a brake second, to judge from what is visible – and the wrong way round too, with the brake compartment facing into the train. Bulleid open second (ex-third) no. 1456 is at the rear of an incoming service, the set number 295 being visible on the extended bodyside panel; from one of the*

Editorial Introduction

Welcome to the first of the 2011 issues of 'Southern Way'. I have to admit that whilst writing this piece (in late September 2010) I was still not quite sure what would be included and what would have to be, regretfully, held over for next time. Sometimes there are valid practical reasons for so doing, space being the obvious, but on occasions when the 'behind the scenes' costs of a particular issue exceed our quota, we have to be a 'bit careful'. That said, a quick flick through the pages of No 13 may give the impression it is all accidents and disasters, but take a closer look and the situation is far from it. Allan Cobb might also have been entitled 'The Life and Times' whilst the Kent Coast piece is fascinating in the way the railway shook itself down and simply got on with the job. Enquiries and collective discussion came later, the priority was to get the traffic moving and minimise inconvenience. You will gather where this could be leading so I will say no more on that topic. Returning though to the theme of accidents and let me say none of us, contributors or editor have any wish to glorify or gloat on the misfortunes of those involved. As one, like unfortunately many, who have been the innocent victim in a road accident, I know only too well the shock and trauma involved. I cannot pretend to imagine the situation for those at Sevenoaks.

Producing a quarterly 'bookazine' (can I interest the lexicographers in a potential new word?) there are advantages and disadvantages so far as content is concerned. You will be aware the intention has always been to try and cover a broad cross section of interest: yes, I freely admit a few pieces are by myself, but I have neither the time and certainly not the knowledge to produce everything on my own. Contributions are therefore always welcome.

One of the advantages of a quarterly product, indeed any regular journal, is that follow-up items can be incorporated: such as in this issue with 'Push-Pull' (I am never sure if it should be 'Pull-Push', both terms appear equally used.). We can also (try to) respond to current interest topics and for this reason keep a watching brief on the various model and discussion groups in an attempt to ascertain what is currently favourite. Even so it is still impossible to be aware of everything, so this is a request not made before, if you have, or can think of a topic we have not covered and perhaps should, please advise us. The LSWR low-pressure pneumatic signalling has already been suggested and this is indeed something we would love to feature. (I did a piece on the trial installation at Grateley many years ago, I think in BRILL, but what is needed is something on the main line.) We have also had suggestions on Crystal Palace, the never completed SR lines of the 1930s, the R1 tank engines and Private Owner wagons in the southern area. All are relevant and whilst for all 'files have been started' there is, as yet, insufficient to proceed. Other items, notably the SR Diesel Shunter types are waiting in the wings for time to complete. We hope also to one day produce a comprehensive work on the SR Electric Locos.

But fashions and tastes change rapidly and in planning a quarterly publication it is difficult, if not impossible, sometimes to alter items at the last minute. Our distributors require notification of new titles and a rough idea of content at least six months ahead. It is for that reason that I suspect some may have been disappointed over an anticipated piece that has yet to appear. Everyone has been very polite on this score and for that I thank you, but as with most specialist railway publishers in the 21st century, the work is usually down to one or two people. Indeed apart from Ian Allan, I know of no other railway publisher that has more staff than can be counted on the fingers of one hand. Which also leads to another point, where does this type of specialist publishing go in the future? Please, this is not meaning to sound depressive, but none of us, readers and editors are getting any younger. I know from my own experience, the further back in history one goes with a topic the less market there is for that product. Equally how many more books are needed on the subject of........... (I have deliberately not mentioned any specific title here). It could well be a new book comes out on say, and to use a generalisation, 'Southern Stations' and containing perhaps 30 or 40 new images. But if there was already a book on the same topic available before does that limited amount of new material warrant a purchase? Finance and shelf space have yet to be considered.

I and sure, and indeed hope, that many like me in railway publishing will keep going for some time to come, perhaps in the end both us as publishers and our market will slowly fade away together. There will of course always be an interest in railways, but perhaps in future that interest will be sated by means of e-books and the like. That is not an area I personally intend to explore. Like many I have spoken to, we desire the tangible product. E-books and readers have their place, as indeed does all technology. But surely the message is that this technology should serve us and not that we should become a slave to it.

Away from the soapbox, it is with great pleasure that we welcome Phillip Atkins and Mike King as contributors to this issue (I hope I have not left anyone else out!). Both will need no introduction, their respective knowledge in the fields of locomotive history and SR rolling stock respectively is beyond reproach. I hope we can persuade them to produce further items in the future.

As ever, thank you for your support. I would be interested to receive your comments on my earlier thoughts. (You will all also notice a few more pages than usual in this issue, we have tried to do a bit of catching up, but there is still a long way to go.)

Kevin Robertson

editorial@thesouthernway.co.uk

(Despite the extra pages in this issue, we apologise that certain items, including one on LSWR lorries and more on Woking Homes has had to be held over to Issue 14.)

Bournemouth line 6-coach sets – and also most definitely not in its correct position in the middle of the set. Officially, this coach was running in special traffic set 212 by mid-1964, so this might give a clue to the date. Today the coach awaits restoration on the Bluebell Railway. For further details of the BR Mk1 coaches allocated to the Southern Region since 1951, turn to page 7. turn to page 7. *Denis Tillman*

Rear Cover - *Almost every heritage railway relies heavily on Mk1 vehicles. This is corridor second S25446 as restored to green livery on the Kent & East Sussex Railway in 2009 – not that it ever carried SR livery, being delivered new in maroon to the LMR in 1957. Despite this being the most common BR Mk1 design (with over 2200 examples) only 27 were originally allocated to the Southern Region, with another 25 or so transferred later.* Mike King

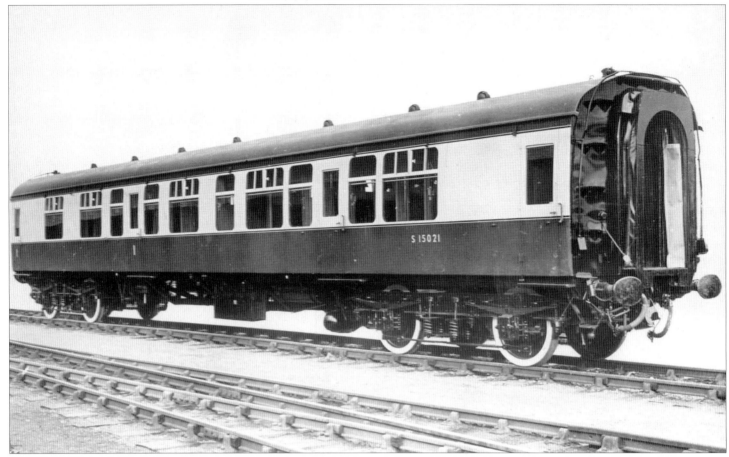

Top - *An official photograph of 'Royal Wessex' composite S15021 when new, in the full glory of lined crimson lake and cream livery. Notice the very square door droplight openings – a feature of the early Mk1's - these proved very susceptible to corrosion. Later vehicles had openings with more radiused corners and later still doors moulded in GRP (glass reinforced plastic). This was one of the coaches exhibited at Marylebone station in March 1951.*

Left - *For many years, 'Royal Wessex' corridor first S13003 was the only such vehicle allocated to the Southern Region. Complete with train name boards at cantrail level, the coach is seen in the rake at Clapham Junction on 21 September 1951. Structurally similar restaurant first S9 is visible to the right.*

D. Cullum 1106, courtesy the Lens of Sutton Association

BR STANDARD Mk 1 STOCK ON THE SOUTHERN REGION 1951 - 1967.

Part 1: 'WESSEX': THE FOUR COACH SETS OF 1952: THE THREE COACH SETS OF 1954 - 1957: NON-CORRIDOR STOCK.

Mike King

Variety, so they tell us, is the spice of life. And so it was for carriage stock enthusiasts on the Southern Region after Nationalisation. Between 1945 and 1951 the new Bulleid stock had injected 814 much-needed modern coaches onto Southern services and these could be seen working alongside pre-Grouping stock already up to 50 years old – sometimes even in the same train. Despite this programme of new-build, thanks to the wartime lack of construction, more carriages were still needed and over the period 1951-67 a further 650 British Railways standard Mk 1 passenger vehicles were added to the region's stock. There were many more similar electric vehicles added from 1956 onwards, but for this article we will concentrate on the locomotive-hauled vehicles. The steady arrival of these, coupled with retrenchment, closures and electrification saw off the last pre-Grouping stock outside the Isle of Wight, surprisingly as late as 1962, while by late 1964 most Maunsell coaches had gone the same way, leaving a combination of Bulleids and BR standards to see out steam in July 1967 – rather mirroring the motive power situation, too.

In some ways the arrival of the new stock had political overtones; the newly-Nationalised industry being at pains to introduce new products that bore little or no obvious pre-nationalisation affinities and could also be distributed throughout the entire railway network. Development and construction were spread across a number of the railway workshops (and outside contractors, too), with Eastleigh taking a share in the work, alongside Swindon, Derby, York, etc., all overseen by a plethora of committees. The various trade unions were also fully consulted about many aspects of design, particularly with regard to internal fittings and finishes. Overall, the works were co-ordinated by the Carriage Standards Committee, which began meeting as early as April 1948. Readers wishing to find out more of the technical details are advised to consult 'British Railways Mark One Coaches' by Keith Parkin and published by the Historical Model Railway Society.

One of the earliest decisions taken by the committee relates to overall dimensions and body profile of the new stock and it was here that Bulleid influence was most obvious. The new vehicles were to be almost identical at 64ft 6in over body (63ft 5in over headstocks) and 9ft wide, while several proposed designs utilised almost the same body layout as found on Bulleid stock. In terms of both body and underframe construction, changes were more apparent. The body structure was now to be all steel (Bulleid coaches used a composite steel and timber construction) and the underframe featured a central girder-like structure capable of withstanding end loads three times greater than a Bulleid coach. These two factors would consign the Bulleid stock to a premature grave in the 1960s, long before they were life-expired, as concern was raised about their performance in the event of an accident. To illustrate this, many Maunsell's gave 30+ years service, not one Bulleid loco-hauled coach managed more than 22. The bogie, designated BR1, was also redesigned on an 8ft 6in wheelbase (6in longer than the SR standard bogie) but although this gave a good ride when new, it deteriorated in service, causing BR to fit many coaches with the heavy (and expensive) cast "Commonwealth" bogie before the designers perfected the B4 bogie suitable for sustained high speed running; but this was not until 1963 and relatively few Mk 1 coaches were ever equipped with them prior to 1967. Catering vehicles were often provided with the BR2 bogie – with stronger springing and dampers to counteract the greater weight of these vehicles.

In terms of livery, most corridor vehicles would appear in lined crimson lake and cream (this was the official description, not carmine and cream, as is so often quoted), although a few full brakes and all the non-corridors had lined crimson – later plain crimson – when new and this was one area where pre-Nationalisation affinities could be claimed to be neutral. "Blood and custard" was the slang applied to the livery and it could vary from one works to another, particularly with regard to the crimson. It was a bright livery for post-war austerity Britain but it failed to wear well in the smoke-laden air of the 1950s and would cease to be applied during 1956. After this time, the regions were allowed more freedom to choose their own liveries and the Southern (predictably) returned to green – of a rather darker shade than used prior to 1949 – whilst lined maroon became standard elsewhere, save for some vehicles for prestige WR services which returned to chocolate and cream. There was talk of the Eastern Region similarly employing mock teak but, if applied, was confined only to experiments. A new number series, commencing at one, with the regional operating prefix (S, W, M, E, SC plus a few GE and NE later) was applied as appropriate - and coaches almost invariably changed prefixes if transferred from one region to another. This could lead to confusion, as pre-Nationalisation vehicles could carry the same number, so from 1951 these had the regional suffix letter added as well. To illustrate the point, S1850 was a mini-buffet allocated to the Southern

Region, whilst S1850S was a Maunsell corridor third dating from 1935. Unless stated to the contrary, all vehicles described in this article carried S prefixes only.

The set numbers applied, however, were not in a new series but these joined the same numbering range used for all SR fixed set formations since 1924 – the series beginning at one and originally reaching 999. The new sets were simply slotted into convenient gaps in the series – very often following on from the last Bulleid sets and this arrangement continued until early 1966 – after which withdrawals and changes to SR-built stock became so frequent that the fixed set formations were suspended for the final two summers of steam operation. By this time most stock was on Waterloo-Bournemouth-Weymouth and Salisbury services but the loss of the set system did contribute to some rather untidy train formations towards the end, especially once a smattering of maroon transfers and newly-repainted blue and grey coaches began to appear. No ordinary Maunsell or Bulleid loco-hauled passenger coaches received blue and grey, but it is rumoured that a few Mk 1's did receive plain blue at Eastleigh in early 1966 (just like the first Bournemouth line electrics) but the author has been unable to verify this. Repainting of this nature always took time, but few blood and custard coaches could still be seen by 1962, while the author last saw a green Mk 1 coach in service in 1969 – at Chester! However, what is believed to be the last railway-owned green Mk 1 was composite 15903, which as departmental RDB975429 could still be seen at Derby in 1984 – and looking reasonably presentable. There is little doubt that green was a hardwearing colour and particularly suited to the rigours of railway operation – not that the author is biased, of course!

One of the first prototypes to be completed (at Eastleigh) in 1950 was composite no. 15000. The production of this vehicle was well documented in photographs (available at a price from the Lancing collection at the NRM) and it was used as a test-bed for a number of new features. Five years earlier the prototype Bulleid composite (S5751S) was used similarly and had what subsequently became the standard Bulleid composite layout of 3 x 3rd class and 4 x 1st class compartments. This coach had been exhibited at a number of locations when new and passengers were invited to fill in a questionnaire giving their views on the interior. Some passengers expressed a preference for open rather than compartment accommodation and, whilst some open third saloons had been provided in production Bulleid stock, no open firsts had been built. The Eastleigh staff must have consulted these questionnaires again, as coach 15000 was initially completed with a unique mix of open and compartment accommodation for both classes. As built, the internal layout was as follows:

End vestibule, lavatory, 3rd, 3rd, 1st, cross-vestibule, 2-bay open 3rd, 2 bay open 1st, lavatory and end vestibule.

In order to accommodate this layout the window positions were varied accordingly to suit the compartment dimensions, making this coach unique, even when it finally entered normal service in 1952 with an orthodox 3 x 3rd and 4 x 1st class compartment layout. As finally running, two first class compartments were of a non-standard third class width (6ft 7in) while lucky third class passengers in one other compartment got 7ft 2in between partitions. The reason why the part open/part compartment layout was

abandoned does not seem to have been recorded, but perhaps it was simply due to the need for the stock to conform to other vehicles already running – to simplify seat reservation arrangements. Interestingly, one type of coach recommended for construction by the Carriage Standards Committee in 1948 – the open composite – was never built and all production Mk 1 corridor composites followed their Bulleid counterparts almost exactly, save for an additional access door on the corridor side. Most other production vehicles (built elsewhere than Eastleigh) mirrored their prototype coaches exactly, save for the addition of a cross-vestibule in the open thirds and firsts. It should also be noted here that third class was redesignated second class in June 1956, but this was a change purely of terminology as with but one exception (to be described later) no physical changes were made to the coaches themselves.

With the basic design parameters now worked out, construction could commence in earnest – or at least as fast as steel supplies would allow – remember this was still post-war austerity Britain. Again, with railway politics in mind it was decided that each region would first receive a complete train of Mk 1 vehicles, together with a newly named service for them to run on. These became known as the "Festival of Britain" trains as their introduction co-incided with the South Bank exhibition. The Southern's was "The Royal Wessex", as it ran between Weymouth and Waterloo and could immediately be connected with the areas described in Thomas Hardy's novels, receiving a complete train of 13 brand-new Mk1's. The stock and the name might have been new, but the train itself revived the "Bournemouth Limited" of pre-war days, commencing at Weymouth at around 7.30am, picking up a Swanage and a Bournemouth West portion en route, arriving at Waterloo around 3¼ hours later. The return journey left at 4.35pm, serving the same destinations, giving an arrival in Bournemouth just before 7pm, Swanage and Weymouth about an hour later. It was therefore possible to make an albeit long day trip to London from Dorset – but just how many commuters made the journey regularly in 1951 is not known – but doubtless far fewer than do so nowadays. The train formation was as follows:

Weymouth portion:	Brake 3rd	34157
	Corridor 3rd	24169
	Composite	15023
	Composite	15021
	Brake 3rd	34158
Swanage portion:	Composite	15022
	Brake 3rd	34155
Bournemouth West portion:	Brake 3rd	34159
	Diner 3rd	1006
	Kitchen car	80009
	Diner 1st	9
	Corridor 1st	13003
	Brake 3rd	34156

BR STANDARD Mk 1 STOCK ON THE SOUTHERN REGION

Notice the large amount of luggage space provision in the five brake coaches and no less than three coaches devoted to catering – both were to result in later changes. Motive power was originally provided by Bournemouth shed in the form of a light pacific selected from the 34093-5/105-110 series and not, surprisingly for the load, a 'Merchant Navy' (none were allocated to Bournemouth in 1951). For this reason punctuality was not always good and in later years a "Packet" became the usual motive power. The generous catering provision was soon found to be unnecessary and a Bulleid "Tavern" pair plus loose BR open third 3914 (not reserved for dining passengers) were substituted. The displaced catering triple found some use on other Bournemouth-Waterloo services during the week and could sometimes be found on Waterloo-Ilfracombe trains at summer weekends, running down on a Saturday and returning on Sundays, but by 1960 the three were running separately on a variety of services. In 1962 the entire train was replaced by Bulleid stock, thereby increasing the passenger accommodation, so patronage must have increased since 1951. The displaced Mk1s then appeared in other sets, including 3-coach formations 572-4, to be described later.

From a modellers viewpoint, a 13-coach train might have its limitations so unless you are modelling the Swanage branch few will be able to make much use of this formation, however a year later a batch of 26 four-coach sets appeared from Eastleigh Works, as follows:

Set No.	Brake 3rd	Corridor 3rd	Composite	Brake 3rd	Date Built
866 to 891	34233 odd nos. to 34283	24302 to 24327	15024 to 15049	34234 even nos. to 34284	March 1952 to Nov 1952.

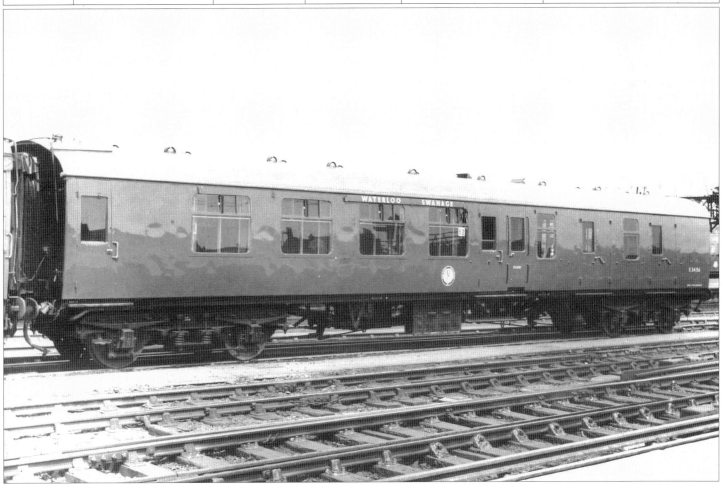

By early 1957 the "Wessex" stock had been repainted in Southern Region green complete with carriage stock crests. Brake third (now second) S34156 is at Clapham Junction, coupled to a Bulleid composite and roof boarded for the Swanage portion of the train. Some swapping around has taken place, as this coach was originally part of the Bournemouth West portion.

R. K. Blencowe collection

Initially, sets 866-76 were for SE Division services (London-Ramsgate/Margate/Dover) and sets 877-91 were for SW Division services (Waterloo-West of England/Bournemouth/Weymouth). Several sets were augmented up to 6-8 coaches with Maunsell or Bulleid stock for specific services, especially for the duration of the summer timetables, while set 872 was deleted in 1954, the centre coaches joining set 873 making this up to at least 6 vehicles on a more permanent basis. Sets 880/85/89 were regularly made up to 8+ vehicles for inter-regional trains and once repainted green after 1956 gave some livery variation when seen in the north of England or at Cardiff. It should be noted that some of these additional coaches were green, even when the Mk1s were in blood and custard prior to that date! The other sets remained in their original formations until 1962 when the corridor thirds (now seconds) were removed, leaving them to run as 3-coach sets until

1965/6 – then joining the pool of other 3-coach sets – by then the most common formation on the region. Another point worth mentioning here is that the third class compartments on Southern (and Western) Region Mk1's seated four-a-side with no intermediete armrests, while those running elsewhere in the country seated three-a-side, with armrests that could (grudgingly!) be raised at busy times to provide additional capacity.

Next in order of appearance were some loose vehicles (mostly open saloons) for boat trains and strengthening purposes, but more about these later. In 1954 the first of 60 three-coach sets began to appear, eventually being allocated set numbers 515-574 and so became the most numerous BR standard formations on the region. They were not delivered in numerical order, so are best summarised by original formations in the following table:

Set No.	Brake 3rd	Composite	Brake 3rd	Date Built	Original Allocation
515	35014	15914	35015	12 / 56	SW Division
516 to 519	35016 even nos. to 35022	15902 to 15905	35017 odd nos. to 35023	1/ 57	SW Division
520	34631	15000	34632	11 / 54	SE Division
521 to 531	34633 odd nos. to 34653	15563 to 15573	34634 even nos. to 34654	5 / 55 to 7 /5 5	SE Division
532 to 540	34613 odd nos. to 34629	15574 to 15582	34614 even nos. to 34630	7 / 55 to 8 / 55	SE Division
541 to 558	34934 even nos. to 34968	15871 to 15888	34935 odd nos. to 34969	10 / 56 to 1 / 57	SE Division
559	35010	15912	35011	12 / 56	'Man of Kent' service
560	35012	15913	35013	12 / 56	'Man of Kent' service
561 to 571	34970 even nos. to 34990	15889 to 15899	34971 odd nos. to 34991	1 / 57 to 4 / 57	SW Division
572	34992	15900	34993	4 / 57	Disbanded by 6 / 57
572	34156	15023	34157	Formed 1962	Ex 'Wessex' stock
573	34158	15022	34159	Formed 1962	Ex 'Wessex' stock
574	34155	15021	34246	Formed 1962	Ex 'Wessex' stock

'Royal Wessex' kitchen car S80009, seen when ex-works and to judge from the surrounding LNER stock in teak/brown, still in the vicinity of Doncaster in 1951, en route for the Southern Region. The white opaque glazing merges with the cream upper panels of the coach. Despite being repainted green by about 1960, the coach saw little use thereafter and was scrapped in 1964. The choice of fuel for these early kitchen cars was anthracite.

Author's collection

Sets 520 and the original 572 were disbanded by June 1957; indeed set 572 may never have run in the form shown above, as the coaches were allocated to sets 427 and 880 by that date. Set 520 also included the prototype composite 15000 that, since entering service in 1952, had previously been the only loose BR standard composite coach on the region. During this time it appears to have run only on the SE Division. Incidentally, this was one of very few Mk1s to carry "left-hand end" numbering. It is also thought that almost all sets listed above appeared in crimson lake and cream from new.

Not surprisingly, with such a large number of sets, quite a few failed to retain their original formations for very long. Sets 515-19/25/40/48/51/60-71 were all noted made up to between 5 and 8 vehicles at various times, usually for the duration of the summer or for a specific duty such as the Brighton-Plymouth service. Many of the additions were Maunsell or Bulleid vehicles and by no means all matched the rest of the set in terms of livery either. Champion amongst these was probably 517, which on peak days between 1962 and 1965 could reach 12 vehicles for the Channel Islands boat express. Some examples of longer formations will be given in part 2.

As time went on there was a general migration towards the SW Division as electrification spread, but some sets in the 532-551 group were retained by the SE Division after electrification for use on various loco-hauled services such as overnight newspaper trains and on the few routes that had failed to receive the third rail and these were equipped with electric heating – a modification applied to all the stock post 1967. Some of these were reformed during 1964/5 with just one brake coach in the centre, flanked by a composite and an open second or in a few cases by two open seconds. This type of formation (with the brake coach positioned anywhere but at the end of the set) was then unusual but has since become commonplace. The displaced brakes then ran as loose vehicles before being incorporated into other sets. Details of these reformations are as follows:

Set No.	Date	Open 2nd	Brake 2nd	Composite	Notes
541	1964	4030	34935	15871	In 1965 SO 4907 replaced CK
542	1964	4037	34936	15872	In 1965 SO 5024 replaced CK
543	1964	4911	34938	15873	In 1965 SO 4910 replaced CK
544	1964	4039	34941	15874	In 1965 SO 4915 replaced CK
545	1964	4908	34942	15875	SO listed in CWN's as 4909
546	1964	4032	34944	15876	CWN =
547	1964	4900	34947	15877	Carriage
549	1964	4040	34950	15879	Working
550	1964	4913	34953	15880	Notice

Set 548 was excluded as this was running as an 8-coach formation at this time. Other locations that saw these sets included the Oxted line and Reading-Guildford-Redhill-Tonbridge services. Some other sets, including 523/26/27/29/36/56/57/59/70 acquired Bulleid composites in place of BR standard ones at this time, the displaced composites being required to make up further long sets formed entirely of Mk1 vehicles, no doubt as a prelude to the mass withdrawal of the Bulleid stock in 1967/8.

Non-Corridor stock

Now would be a good moment to consider these rather interesting (and fairly elusive) vehicles. The BR standard non-corridors were built mostly on short (56ft 11in) underframes and were most often found on the Metropolitan widened lines into Moorgate – being allocated to LMR and ER outer suburban services. A small number were built on the longer underframes for the Western and Southern Regions. The first to be received by the Southern were four 3-coach sets (Nos. 152-55) for the Exeter-Exmouth branch, delivered in early 1956 in plain unlined crimson livery. By 1955 this intensively worked commuter line held a great variety of vintage LSWR corridor and non-corridor coaches, often hauled by equally veteran M7 tanks, up to 7 coaches in a train. The new sets were as follows:

Set No.	Brake 3rd	Composite	Brake 3rd
152 to 155	43374 even nos. to 43380	41060 to 41063	43375 odd nos. to 43381

There was to have been set 156, numbered in sequence but the coaches for this were diverted to Oxted line set 904 instead, where similar overcrowding was being experienced. To work with these coaches 19 ten-compartment thirds (nos. 46280-98) were provided, allowing Exmouth branch trains to run with a maximum of six coaches (3-set plus three strengtheners). With their 6-a-side seating, this equalled or exceeded the previous 7-coach LSWR rakes. At rush hours, this was a necessary provision, too. The coaches remained at Exeter (in green livery by about 1960) until WR takeover and subsequent DMU provision during 1963, after which a few of the thirds (now seconds) returned to the Southern Region for redeployment. During their stay in the west of England the thirds did turn up on the Sidmouth, Seaton and Lyme Regis branches, even at Plymouth or Salisbury on main line stoppers on occasions.

The coaches intended for set 156 were, as already mentioned, reallocated to the Oxted line for commuter set 904, formed as below:

Set No.	Brake 3rd	3rd	Composite	Lav. Composite	3rd	Brake 3rd
904	43382	46297	41064	S4727S	46298	43383

Five of the coaches were clearly from the intended Exmouth branch batches, but the lavatory composite was a real gem – an ex-LSWR 58ft rebuild on a 1935 Southern underframe. Just whether the first class passengers from Tunbridge Wells preferred the comfort of the old LSWR vehicle or the spartan first class compartments in the BR composite could be debated – but undoubtedly the BR non-corridor first comfort was a bit lacking! The LSWR coach was replaced by two Bulleid corridor composites during 1958 (nos. S5890/91S) and in turn by Mk1 composites 16202/3 in 1965 – these having come from the Western Region. The author saw the set being whisked rapidly through Clapham Junction by a Crompton in 1964, formed with just the five non-corridors in green livery.

Returning to set 156, this did eventually become a noncorridor Mk1 formation, but in a gradual manner. It was formed in 1959 for the West London line (Clapham Junction-Kensington Olympia) service and originally comprised one Maunsell Thanet brake flanked by two SECR seconds on either side. By 1963 this had become a later Maunsell brake plus three former Exmouth branch BR seconds, as below: -

Coach S1000S was completed at Eastleigh in 1962 as a ten-compartment second, having a pre-finished green glass fibre reinforced plastic body built on the underframe of open second 4377, which had been destroyed in the St Johns rear-end collision on 4th December 1957. This was a form of construction with which Eastleigh was then pioneering and whilst complete bodies did not progress much further, manufacture of doors and many smaller components most certainly did so. The coach had first entered service in the Lancing works train, then numbered as departmental DS70200, but was soon given a traffic department number in the former SR series (with S-suffix to denote its "non-standardness") and transferred to the Hayling Island branch until closure in November 1963. It then moved to Clapham Junction and remained on the "Kenny Belle" until the end of steam in July

Set No.	2nd	2nd	Brake 2nd	2nd	Date	Notes
156	46284	46290	S4235S	46294	1962 / 3	Maunsell 1936 Brake
156	46291	46292	S4210S	46293	1964	Bulleid BRCW Brake
156	46292	46293	S4372S	S1000S	1965	Bulleid Brake Coach

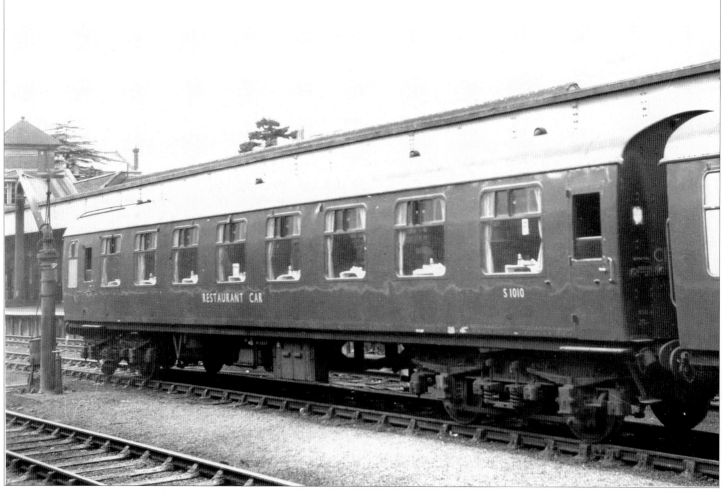

Restaurant third (now second) S1010 arrived on the Southern Region from the Western in 1962 but was identical to 'Wessex' car 1006. The coach is coupled to Mk1 buffet/restaurant S1721, just visible at the right, and a Bulleid brake composite at Exeter Central on 23 August 1963 and will be shunted into the centre of the next up express for Waterloo. Note that BR2 bogies are fitted and that replacement externally beaded window frames have been provided.

A. E. West R4382

BR STANDARD Mk 1 STOCK ON THE SOUTHERN REGION

1967 – the train's claim to fame being the last steam-worked suburban service in the south of England. The author saw the set elsewhere just once; on 1st August 1964 it was in the down carriage sidings at Woking and was used on a Basingstoke local on that high-summer Saturday. The coach was subsequently retained for further use (seemingly never instigated) and was stored at Micheldever and Eastleigh before being purchased for preservation in 1973 and today runs on the East Somerset Railway – probably the only surviving long-frame BR standard non-corridor coach – fundamentally if not obviously different to all other BR non-corridors.

Perhaps surprisingly, the Southern Region acquired some more non-corridor seconds in 1964-66. In anticipation of the Bournemouth electrification and the promise of a better commuter train service from stations west of Woking, the housebuilders had got busy and this was beginning to overwhelm the few steam-hauled commuter trains serving Farnborough, Fleet, Winchfield and Hook, so 11 former WR seconds were drafted in for use on these trains. Numbers involved were 46005/8/22/23/31/35/39/59 and 46273-5. All received S prefixes

(rather hastily by the look of some of them) and whilst a few were overhauled and repainted green, several retained somewhat worn lined maroon livery to the end. At the risk of being uncharitable, no doubt some of these were either due for shopping or had already been withdrawn by the Western Region – they were not likely to part with useful coaches in good condition! These were incorporated into some of the Basingstoke commuter trains, together with a few of the (now green) former Exmouth seconds, resulting in greater capacity – if not comfort! The author's only experience of one was in an up stopper from Salisbury to Surbiton in August 1964. We merrily piled into the leading compartment of a pair of maroon vehicles behind a Guildford-allocated standard mogul but by the first stop at Porton had had enough and decided to switch into the Bulleid 3-set forming the rest of the train! The coaches remained in use until July 1967, all subsequently going for scrap.

Part 2 will deal with the loose vehicles, longer sets, catering and non-passenger coaching stock.

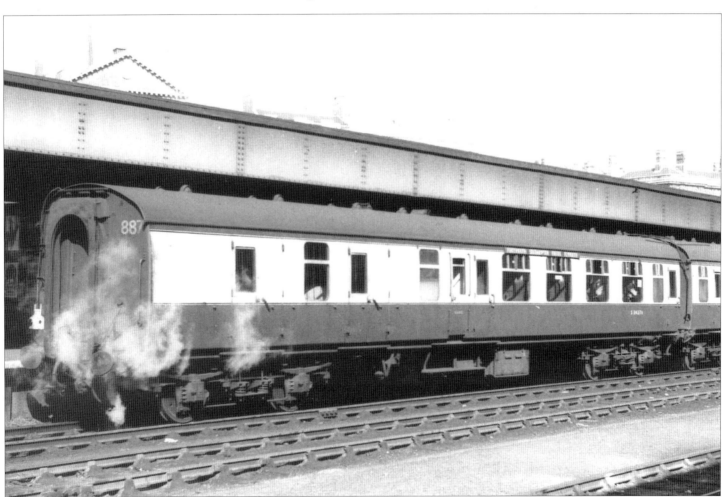

Brake third S34276 of 4-set 887 leaving Exeter Central at the rear of the Plymouth-Brighton express punctually at 1pm on 14 March 1961, still carrying 'blood and custard' livery. The roof boards read 'Portsmouth Southampton Exeter Plymouth' while the Brighton portion at the front was formed of 6-set 516. Steam heating is evident – the presence of which exacerbated any corrosion problems in these vehicles.

A. E. West R3517

Above - *Brake third S35015 of set 515 at Salisbury when new in late 1956 or early 1957, proving that most, if not all, of the 3-sets were outshopped in crimson lake and cream. This has been augmented to six vehicles with Bulleids and a Maunsell buffet car, all in green livery. The BR route restriction (C1) has been applied but a Southern Region Restriction 4 plate is also visible on the coach end.*

N. C. Simmons

Opposite top - *Exmouth branch non-corridor second S46285 in green livery at Sidmouth Junction on 10 June 1963. Whereas 3-coach sets 152-5 seldom left the Exmouth branch, the loose seconds could wander around the West of England and the author has photographic evidence of them at Lyme Regis, Seaton, Callington and Plymouth during the 1956-64 period.*

A. E. West R4232

Opposite bottom - *The plastic-bodied coach S1000S at the rear of a West London line service at Clapham Junction on 10 May 1966. Superficially, the coach resembles a normally constructed second, but there are subtle detail differences such as the wrap-around roof at the end and rounded body corners. Note also the very clean-looking roof. Bulleid semi-open brake second S4372S is just visible to the right.*

H. C. Casserley 114052

Top - *Ashford Works official portrait of three cylinder 2-6-0 No. 822 as newly completed in December 1922, and thereby (briefly) carrying an SE&CR plate on the cabside. The entire engine presents an extremely tidy piece of design work, due largely to William Hooley. Note the forward extension rods from the outside Walschaerts valve gear to operate in the derived valve gear for the middle piston valve, a notably superior arrangement to that found on the corresponding Gresley three cylinder 2-6-0s on the GNR. Regrettably inside Walschaerts valve gear (operated by two eccentrics) was substituted in 1931. In a letter to the writer, Harold Holcroft claimed that this had been merely to bring 822 'into line' with the five production N1s built in 1930 (Nos.A876-880), and that his valve gear had in fact been 'quite satisfactory' for eight years. As BR No. 31822 this very interesting locomotive was withdrawn from service in November 1962, ironically exactly coincident with the publication of Holcroft's 'Locomotive Adventure', which contained an arrangement drawing of its original valve gear layout.*

Left - *The portrait of W G Hooley, probably taken several years earlier (from the style of the tie worn this would indicate the 1920's), which accompanied his obituaries published in February 1936.*

16

THE MAN WHO *REALLY* DESIGNED THE MAUNSELL 'MOGULS'

Philip Atkins

It is now nearly fifty years since the publication of the late Harold Holcroft's memoirs, in which he described his work in the locomotive departments of successively the Great Western, South & Eastern & Chatham and Southern railways.[1] This brought him into close personal contact with such luminaries as George Churchward, Richard Maunsell and Oliver Bulleid. However, he was probably the first to dispel the popular myth that steam locomotives had been *personally* designed by the chief mechanical engineers to whom by tradition they were accredited.

Having said this, in *Locomotive Adventure* Holcroft made but two passing references to one W G Hooley, remarking that 'he it was who had done all the preliminary scheming...... of the various (Maunsell locomotive) classes outlined at Waterloo'. On the evidence of Ashford drawing office records, now preserved at the National Railway Museum in York, this did not really do full justice to Hooley because a good ten years earlier, in 1914 when aged only 27, he had been the true architect of the most numerous and enduring Maunsell locomotives, the 2-6-0s. Furthermore, six years later he had done much of the detail design work for the then experimental three cylinder version, whereas Holcroft's narrative appeared to imply that he himself had tackled the job single-handed.

William Glynn Hooley was born in Timperley, Cheshire in 1887 and c.1904 commenced an apprenticeship at Beyer, Peacock & Co., the renowned locomotive builders, at Gorton, in east Manchester, a few miles away. For nearly three years thereafter he functioned as a draughtsman, and entries under his name can be found in the Beyer, Peacock drawing registers between October 1909 and July 1911; there is a distinctly cryptic valedictory in pencil made by a colleague against the final entry. [2] Although no comparable evidence now survives, Hooley thereupon moved across Manchester to take up similar employment with Nasmyth, Wilson & Co. at Patricroft. This was an older but smaller enterprise than Beyer's, whose total locomotive production during 1912 amounted to only 29 locomotives, compared with precisely one hundred at the Gorton Foundry.

It was customary at this period that in order to gain experience, and also promotion, locomotive draughtsmen freely migrated between the drawing offices of the private locomotive builders and those of the main line railways. William Hooley's initials first appear in the drawing register of the Ashford Works of the South Eastern & Chatham Railway in January 1913, at the tail end of the Wainwright regime, when he was appointed as a senior locomotive draughtsman. [3] Happier times had seen the production of the supremely elegant Class 'D' and 'E' 4-4-0s, but now there was a crisis regarding an accumulating backlog of locomotive repairs, and Harry Wainwright's private life was also in disarray. [4] In day to day charge of locomotive design at Ashford was the chief draughtsman, Robert Surtees, a former London, Chatham & Dover man, but a Geordie by birth who had served his time with Robert Stephenson &

Co. in his native Newcastle. (Intriguingly, the census returns for 1861 indicate that at the tender age of five years Surtees had been resident in Hunslet, Leeds, another notable locomotive building district).

Both Wainwright and Surtees took early retirement and were respectively replaced in early 1914 by Richard Maunsell, from the Great Southern & Western Railway in Ireland, and James Clayton from the Midland Railway at Derby. Clayton had also been a Beyer, Peacock 'graduate' and had functioned as a draughtsman there before moving in 1899 to Ashford, where he remained until 1902, before later joining the Midland. He would already have known some of the older draughtsmen, who included Surtees' son, also named Robert. Two Swindon men were also recruited, George Pearson as assistant CME and works manager, and Harold Holcroft from the drawing office as a technical assistant.

No time was wasted in initiating two new locomotive designs, whose first emergence was distinctly delayed until mid-1917 by the tragic turn of international events. Hooley was instructed to scheme a 2-6-4 passenger tank engine with 6ft coupled wheels (advocated by Pearson) and a 2-6-0 mixed traffic/goods tender engine with 5ft 6in wheels to be directly derived from it. Clayton had brought with him from the Midland a newly made diagram for a proposed 2-6-4T for the recently absorbed London, Tilbury & Southend line, having a standard Derby parallel superheated boiler and massive (S&D 2-8-0) 21in. diameter cylinders with short travel valves. This was re-jigged with 19in. cylinders having long travel valves, and a tapered Belpaire boiler with top feed. However, this was *not* strictly in the Swindon style as it had a dome and flat sides to the firebox, and was in fact closely based on a boiler Clayton had sketched out at Derby in c.1911 for proposed 2-10-0 and 0-6-6-0 banking tank engines for the Lickey Incline. [5] Hooley's 2-6-4T diagram was dated 23 June 1914, and that for the corresponding 2-6-0, 16 July 1914. [6] The profiles of the cab, tender and chimney of the 2-6-0 were each pure Derby, no doubt with reference to James Clayton. Initially just one of each is type completed at Ashford just three years later, the 2-6-4T (designated Class 'K') although later multiplied immediately after 1923 by the Southern Railway as the 'River' class, soon achieved considerable notoriety after a series of derailments. The latter culminated in the fatal accident at Sevenoaks in August 1927, and the class was swiftly converted thereafter into nameless 2-6-0 tender engines which retained their 6ft coupled wheels. By contrast, the original 5ft 6in. 2-6-0 design (Class 'N') would remain in continuous service for almost fifty years.

In January 1917 Hooley executed the overall general arrangement drawing for the Class 'N', but between times was also responsible for much more mundane yet still very necessary drawings, for example a 'brake block for road vehicles', reflecting the current war situation, in October 1915. A month later he worked out a scheme to rebuild one of the 110 Wainwright Class C 0-6-0s as a 0

Class 'U' 2-6-0, BR No. 31794 on the Eastleigh turntable in early British Railways days. This engine had started life in May 1925 as 'K' class 2-6-4T No. A794 'River Rother', which had been assembled in Newcastle by Armstrong Whitworth & Co. from parts made at Ashford and Woolwich Arsenal. However, it was rebuilt as a nameless 2-6-0 just three years later, but as such lasted until withdrawn from service in June 1963.

Tony Molyneaux

-6-0ST for shunting duties; No.695 was in due course selected for this unique treatment and emerged in its new guise just two years later.

Hooley does not appear to have been particularly involved with the Clayton-inspired major reconstructions of certain of the Wainwright 'D' and 'E' 4-4-0s, but in May 1919 he produced diagrams for proposed 2-8-0 tanks, again probably at Pearson's behest, which would have incorporated the K/N taper boiler, in both two- and *three*-cylinder versions, which were not mentioned by Holcroft.

While still at Swindon and with Churchward's personal blessing, Holcroft in 1909 had obtained a patent for a derived valve gear to work the middle valve of a three-cylinder locomotive from the movement of the 'outside' valve gears. Several years later, in November 1918, he presented a paper advocating three-cylinder locomotives, to the Institution of Locomotive Engineers in Leeds, which was attended by a representative of Nigel Gresley of the Great Northern Railway. Having very recently completed a three-cylinder 2-8-0 locomotive himself, Gresley invited Holcroft to discuss related issues in his office at King's Cross in January 1919. Richard Maunsell was evidently not best pleased when he later learned of this meeting and declared that he intended to build some three-cylinder locomotives himself. He tasked Holcroft with designing a three-cylinder version of the 'N' 2-6-0 without interference from Clayton. Holcroft stated this directive was immediately afterwards in February 1919, but no related entries began to appear in the drawing registers until a full year later, and then only a single one was ascribed to 'HH', for a pendulum lever, which is actually referred to on p.95 of his book. He described 'taking a clean sheet of paper' and discussing with the foreman of the works foundry the best way to cast the cylinders and they decided to cast the left hand and middle cylinders together as a pair, to which the separately cast right hand cylinder would be bolted. The outside steam chests were to be inclined inwards, Swindon-style, to permit forward extensions from the outside valve gears to work the derived valve gear mounted ahead of the cylinders, in order to avoid incurring expansion errors from the valve spindles.

It was not until August 1920 that *William Hooley* actually made the drawings for the cylinders, together with full size sections thereof for the benefit of the pattern makers, later to be followed by the necessarily modified frame and cab arrangement drawings. No.822 (Class 'N1') was completed as the last SE&CR engine in December 1922, but did not enter service until the following month at the dawn of the Southern Railway era. The 2-6-0 was not a particularly large engine and the incentive to provide it with three (smaller) cylinders was the notably reduced clearances on the Hastings line, more particularly the 'pinch point' presented by the ever troublesome Mountfield Tunnel. This would also later prompt the design of the 'Schools' 4-4-0, but even well before the completion of No.822 a diagram prepared as early as April 1921 showed a three cylinder version of the passenger 2-6-4T in relation to the tunnel, just one of which, No.A890 *River Frome* (Class 'K1'), was later built in early Southern days.

Richard Maunsell was appointed chief mechanical engineer of the Southern Railway, and after 18 months moved with his technical staff to new accommodation at Waterloo Station. William Hooley was promoted to leading locomotive draughtsman and there produced the initial schemes for nearly all the subsequent locomotive designs ascribed to Maunsell. (7) However, unlike the earlier 2-6-0 and 2-6-4T, the final results invariably deviated to a greater or lesser degree from the 'first draft', which Holcroft attributed to Clayton not taking a sufficiently strong line with T S 'Jock' Finlayson, the dour chief draughtsman at Eastleigh.

In October 1924 Hooley produced the initial diagram for the 'Lord Nelson' four cylinder 4-6-0, which showed a cylindrical smokebox resting on a saddle (anathema to Finlayson) and a cab with two side windows. When the prototype duly emerged from Eastleigh Works in 1926 it had a built up smokebox and a different cab, actually more in the Derby style.

Holcroft aptly described the later 'Schools' three cylinder 4-4-0 as a 'three quarter Nelson', and that, although outstanding, as built it departed considerably from Hooley's original scheme of April 1928. That had showed a taper Belpaire boiler and 22 ton ax-

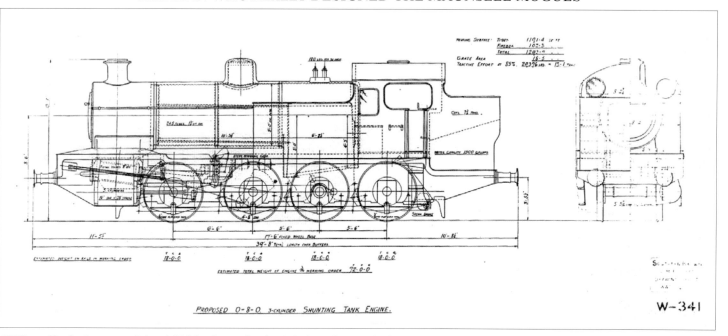

PROPOSED 0-8-0 3-CYLINDER SHUNTING TANK ENGINE.

W-341

William Hooley's original April 1926 scheme for the 'Z' class three cylinder 0-8-0T heavy shunting engine. As built at Brighton three years later, it incorporated three independent sets of valve gear with a consequent shortening of the front overhang, 'bevelled' side tanks to improve forward visibility whilst the outside diameter of the boiler cladding was distinctively increased in diameter relative to that of the smokebox.

The production design. 'Z' No. 30953 outside Templecombe shed May / June 1958.

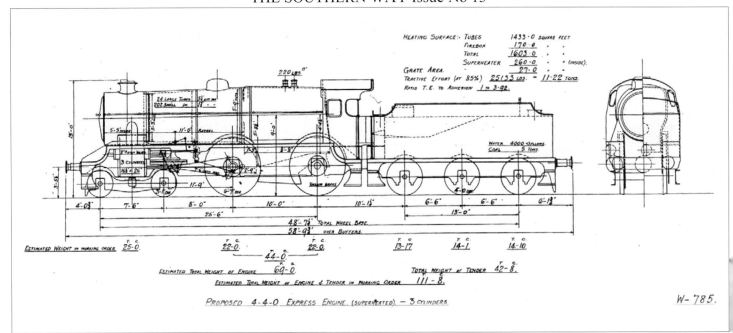

William Hooley's original April 1928 scheme for the Class V or 'Schools' three cylinder 4-4-0 express passenger engine. This showed a tapered Belpaire firebox (with firebox derived from that of the 'Lord Nelson' 4-6-0), cylindrical smokebox, and 22 ton axleload.

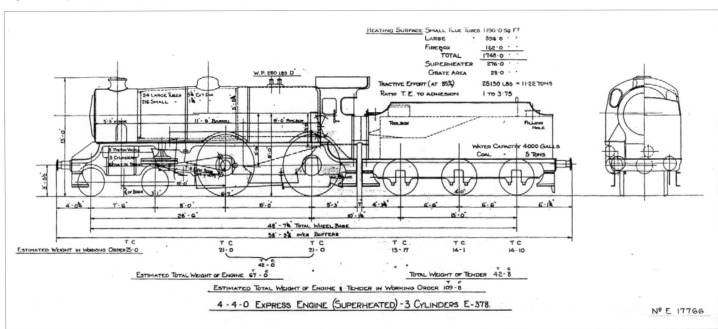

The previously unpublished intermediate Eastleigh three cylinder 4-4-0 scheme, dated August 1928, derived from the above under T S Finlayson, incorporating a shorter, still tapered, version of the round topped 'King Arthur' 4-6-0 boiler, built up smokebox, and 21 ton axleload. As actually built at Eastleigh some 18 months later the final version was very similar except that the boiler barrel was parallel rather than tapered as it had been in the KA.

leload. A subsequent intermediate development at Eastleigh showed a shortened version of the 'King Arthur' round topped boiler, retaining its own tapered barrel, and built up smokebox, with axleload reduced to 21 tons. The final version was similar but simply had a parallel boiler. One would love to have seen how the *original* proposal would have performed, but at least a slightly modified version of its boiler was later employed on the Bullied Q1 0-6-0, although concealed within its unique outer casing.

In April 1926 Hooley produced diagrams for two powerful tank engines incorporating the standard 2 plus 1 cylinder castings and Holcroft's derived valve gear, then only to be found on 2-6-0 No.822 and 2-6-4T No.890. The first was a non-superheated 0-8-0T for heavy shunting duties, but unfortunately the civil engineer objected to the excessive front overhang occasioned by the said valve gear and an inside set of Walschaerts had to be substituted, thereby reducing the overall length by about one foot. Eight such engines of

Class 'Z' were later built at Brighton in 1929, but a projected further batch was later cancelled owing to the economic situation.

The other design was for a 5ft 6in. 2-6-4T, originally entitled 'mixed traffic', which was later re-submitted in 1929 as 'goods', in the wake of the Sevenoaks accident. This would utilise the redundant side tanks and bunkers (after modification) removed from the passenger 2-6-4Ts following their conversion to 2-6-0s, but by the time they were actually built between 1931 and 1936 the derived valve gear had been removed from Nos.822 and 890 and the 'Ws' were likewise turned out with three sets of Walschaerts valve gear.

An 'N' 2-6-0 with 6ft coupled wheels had been schemed by Hooley's colleague R G Hodges as early as January 1925, and the limited operational value of the 2-6-4Ts had already become apparent even before Sevenoaks. Hooley himself produced a scheme in July 1928 for a three cylinder 6ft 2-6-0 for the Hastings line. Both duly appeared as Classes 'U' and 'U1'.

What to do with another class of large passenger tank engines on the Southern Railway later posed a problem. Following the inauguration of the London-Brighton electrification on 1 January 1933, the imposing L B Billinton 4-6-4Ts were initially transferred to Eastbourne, where electrification would duly catch up with them again 18 months later. In anticipation of this Hooley produced a scheme in November 1933 to rebuild them as 4-6-0 tender engines,

which as such would run for a further twenty years or so. In his book, Holcroft claimed to have worked out a similar scheme, but which would have also involved fitting 'King Arthur' boilers, six years earlier, the very day before the Sevenoaks accident, although at that time five of the seven engines were only five/six years old.

What should have been Maunsell's *magnum opus*, the 'Lord Nelson', never quite seemed to give complete satisfaction. Independently of Waterloo, Eastleigh in 1931 produced all the necessary drawings to rebuild one as a four cylinder compound with 250lb boiler, to which Holcroft strangely made no reference. In November 1933 Waterloo for its part produced a diagram for a 'Nelson' with 6ft 3in. coupled wheels expanded into a 4-6-2 with wide firebox, the boiler shell closely resembling those of the Gresley LNER A1/A3s (possibly in the hope that Eastleigh could borrow the press blocks from Doncaster). Somewhat surprisingly, Hooley did not draft this but two months later produced a relatively minor drawing relating to its would-be cylinders. Interest then transferred instead to a three cylinder 2-6-2 (which would remarkably have anticipated the slightly later Gresley V2), which continued well into 1935, by which time Hooley was suffering from serious health problems resulting in his absence from work. Probably because of this, in March 1935 a colleague produced the initial diagram for a 'Proposed 0-6-0 Goods Engine', simply by way of a replacement for the ageing 0-6-0s on

1.9 pm van train to Brighton at London Bridge. 'U1' No. 31891, 13 March 1950.

the Southern, none of which then was less than 25 years old. With a strong hint of the ponderous Derby 4F, even down to the same 8ft + 8ft 6in. coupled wheel spacing (later replicated in the Bulleid 0-6-0s), this became the Class Q introduced in 1938 after Maunsell's retirement.

    William Hooley logged what proved to be his final drawing at Waterloo on 27 November 1935. He died suddenly on 11 January 1936 at the early age of 48, shortly after returning from a period of recuperation at Torquay, having been taken ill on arriving back at his home in Purley, according to his obituary notice in the *Southern Railway Magazine* for February 1936. This was accompanied by a small portrait, which also accompanied a shorter obituary in *The Locomotive Magazine* published the same month. Hooley also appears unidentified (middle row, fourth from right) in a staff group photograph taken at Ashford in 1924 which is reproduced in Holcroft's book.

References

1.   H Holcroft, *Locomotive Adventure*, Ian Allan, 1962

2.   Beyer, Peacock & Co. drawing registers, Beyer, Peacock Archive, Museum of Science and Industry, Manchester

3.   Ashford Works drawing register, Search Engine, National Railway Museum, York

4.   K Marx, *Wainwright and his Locomotives*, Ian Allan, 1985

5.   A F Cook, *Raising Steam on the LMS, - the evolution of LMS locomotive boilers*, Railway Correspondence & Travel Society, 1999 (40-41)

6.   Ashford Works sketch register, Search Engine, National Railway Museum, York.

    Waterloo drawing register, Search Engine, National Railway Museum, York .

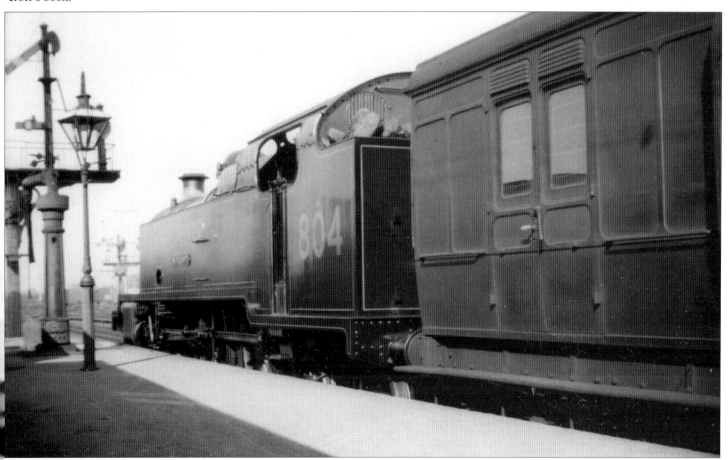

Opposite top - *A rare view of an unidentified three-cylinder Class 'W' 2-6-4T under construction at either Ashford or Eastleigh in the early 1930s. The side tank being lowered into position would have been re-fashioned from one taken from a 'K' class passenger 2-6-4T a few years earlier.*

Opposite bottom - *The class 'W' 2-6-4Ts were arguably the most impressive of the Maunsell 2-6-0 'family;, which also included 2-6-0s in the Irish Republic and (two-cylinder) 2-6-4Ts on the Metropolitan Railway, which were fabricated from surplus 2-6-0 parts made at Woolwich Arsenal. They were also the last Maunsell three cylinder locomotives to remain in service, with some lasting into 1964. No. 1917 is seen in its prime. Although originally authorised in March 1929, it was not finally assembled at Ashford until six years later owing to the very depressed national economy. It was withdrawn from service as BR No. 31917 in January 1964.*

Above - *Except for the prototype No. 790 built in 1917, the Class 'K' 2-6-4Ts ran for very few years before their conversion and so photographs of them are uncommon. No. A804 'River Tamar', seen here in a platform view, only ran as such for barely a year from new in September 1926, before entering storage prior to rebuilding in early 1928. As a 2-6-0 it fared rather better, being withdrawn in June 1964.*

STANDARD 20 H.P CAR. THE DREWRY CAR CO. LTD. 13. SOUTH PLACE. LONDON E.C.

Top - *The Standard 20 HP Drewry Car.*

Author's Collection

Left - *LBSC Inspection car, possibly later 347s at Christ's Hospital.*

Courtesy the Brighton Circle / H M Hoather

Further comment on this fascinating vehicle will appear shortly.

DREWRY INSPECTION CAR No. 346S

Nick Holliday

The drawing in *Southern Way Issue No 11*, showing a 'Drewry' Inspection Car No. 346S, first came to my notice when it appeared in the Summer 2000 issue of the *Brighton Circular*. The problem is how best to reconcile this drawing from 1933, which purports to be 346S, with the various photographs taken of that apparently self-same vehicle after the war, one of which was reproduced in the Winter 2000 Circular. My suspicions were first aroused by the caption to a very clear picture of No. 346S (probably taken at Exmouth in about 1947) in *British Railways Illustrated*, August 1995 issue *(BRILL)*, which mentions the 1933 drawing but suggests that the rebuilding never took place. This photo shows a coach-panelled box on wheels with three doors and windows all round, a far cry from the vintage automobile design of the drawing.

Kidner, in *Service Stock of the Southern Railway* (Oakwood Press 1993), clearly identifies 346S as being built in 1915 by Drewry Works. (Works No. 615)The 'standard' Drewry 20 HP Railway Inspection Car of that era was a very simple affair, with three rows of reversible seats, square radiators at each end and a distinctive curvaceous horn.

The North Staffordshire Railway acquired one such device in 1921, Drewry Works No. 1200, which had a Baguley 20 HP 4 cylinder engine and weighed 1T 12cwt. This, perhaps coincidentally, was shortly after Mr. C G Rose joined the Knotty as Assistant Engineer, having come from Brighton Works. In an article in *Model Railways, April 1975* edition, F W Shuttleworth provided photographs and drawings of it, both as originally acquired, with fetching side curtains, and as subsequently rebuilt with a fully enclosed body, both of which demonstrating many similarities to the photographs of 346s. (Both pictures are also in *North Staffordshire Locomotives* by Ken Hopkins, Trent Valley Publications 1986)

Whilst it would not be totally impossible to take such a basic 'Ugly Duckling' and transform it into the 'swan' of the 1933 scheme, there seems little point in the transformation, which, if anything, would have resulted in a less versatile machine and would appear to use little of the original. It requires an even greater leap of faith to believe that in 1947 the Southern Railway then set about, at Exmouth of all places, to return the machine to look almost exactly the same as when it was built, as

was suggested in an earlier *Circular* article. They even managed to restore the distinctive Drewry horn, clearly visible on the *BRILL* photograph.

There can be no doubt that a vehicle answering vaguely to the same description as the drawing did exist, given the eye-witness accounts. What I do not believe is that it has anything to do with the post-war S346S as photographed. Apart from the number of wheels, the only similarities between the two are their wheelbase and their method of propulsion. The many differences are obvious by comparing the drawing and the various photos of S346S.

However, the drawing had a certain ring of familiarity, and I eventually realised where I had seen the machine in question before. In the Spring 1995 issue of the *Brighton Circular* (Volume 21, Page 14) there was a picture of an inspection car at Christ's Hospital, from the collection of Mr. H Hoather, that was probably taken in the late 20s or early 30s, judging from the dress of the men present. This vehicle, with its distinctive oval radiator, is a dead ringer for that shown in the drawing, except that it is the 'cabriolet' version. I therefore suggest that the 1933 drawing was prepared to show proposals for fully enclosing the device in that photograph - whether the work was done I cannot say.

Meanwhile the original Drewry car was soldiering on. The style of bodywork is redolent of Brighton or Lancing, and I would suggest that the fully enclosed body was fitted either immediately on delivery or very shortly afterwards, certainly before grouping.

It may have received attention at Exmouth in 1947, but I suspect the extent of alterations was minimal. After all, Exmouth was a pre-cast concrete plant, and shuttering hands would be unlikely to turn out such a complex shape, which anyway does not display any LSWR or Southern traits in its design. Indeed, judging by the rippling on several of the body panels, I would suggest that the work consisted of replacing rotten panels with plywood that had been rejected from use in shuttering due to delamination. The BRILL picture shows this rippling even though the finish is relatively pristine. The pictures taken at different times at Stewarts Lane (another one appears in *Clapham Junction – Fifty Years of Change* by Vic Mitchell and Keith Smith - Middleton Press 1998 - Plate 60) show it in a rather derelict state. It

New No.	Old No.	Class	Built by	Date	Date Cond.	Dept.	Remarks
346s	1	(1930) Petrol Car (1923) Insp. Saloon	Drewry	1915	In error 14.4.34	E's	Inspection Car Haywards Heath Eastleigh 9/33 Returned to stock 15.12.34
347s	2	(1930) Petrol Car (1923) Insp. Saloon	Brighton	1912	14.4.34	E's	Inspection Car East Croydon Eastleigh 9/33

No. 346s travelling on the Up South Western line at Wimbledon during the General Strike. Taken by H C Casserley on 8 May 1926.

is hard to imagine that British Railways got another five or six years service out of it, but Kidner reports its only being withdrawal from Redhill in 1954.

To summarise, I would suggest that there were two very different vehicles involved:

1   A basic standard 20 HP Drewry Inspection Car, delivered to Brighton in 1915 and fitted, probably at Lancing, with an enclosed body shortly after. This was then patched up at Exmouth in 1947 and survived until 1954 at Redhill.

2   A prettier, if not very functional, open top car, perhaps on a Riley chassis, as suggested in the 1995 Circular article, photographed at Christ's Hospital and later noted at Southampton and similar to the drawing. It is this vehicle that was the subject of a proposal to fit an all-over body in 1933 but work was probably not carried out. Its ultimate disposal is not known.

I can only assume that there was some confusion regarding the Service Stock numbers of these machines. The Southern had little logic when applying these, although most Central Section stock was numbered in the 300s. Mike King of the Brighton Circle, produced some further information that backed this up; entries from the SR Service stock register; from which it would seem that the two cars were sent to Eastleigh in September 1933 and both were condemned on 14 April 1934, but the Drewry's death sentence was in error, and it was reinstated to stock on 15 December 1934.

It is much easier to reconcile this theory than any suggestion that any dramatic physical transformation(s) actually took place! Certainly 346S was not built at Brighton in 1933, as suggested in *SW*, but it would be useful if someone could identify the mystery source of the petrol car 347s in 1912, as shown in the drawing; that radiator is so distinctive, it should be easy, even though Mike's notes show it as being built at Brighton.

Left - No. 346S at Stewarts Lane. Spring 1949.   Brighton Circle
***Opposite page** - Our recent pictorial coverage of Ventnor West (SW11) and book 'Memories of Isle of Wight Railways', has generated much comment of late. To continue this interest, another previously unpublished view, from 1948 of the same location. 'Terrier' No. 13, formerly identified as No. W3 and carrying the name 'Carisbrooke', attending to 'engine requirements', both liquid and from the look of the smoke, solid, at the end of the platform. The photographer comments, "I cannot recall if they took on water before arriving, with the few passengers forced to wait, or reversed back." Probably the latter.*
Henry Meyer

SOUTHERN RAILWAY
WARNING

Not No. 34067 and not 2009, but does it matter, we think not. Reported as a West of England working in 1931 and captioned "Three modes of transport". I could not possibly comment on which might be preferred.

Charles Brown

WESTWARD HO! - IN RETROSPECT

(Southern Region Engineman)

James (Jim) Lester 70A

On Sunday 5 July 2009 I made my way to my local station at Woking and arrived at 8.45 am. The purpose of my mission was, if possible, to turn the clock back to the early `sixties and experience once again mainline steam down the Exeter road, this time back on the footplate.

What actually occurred when I joined the footplate and the crew of 'Battle of Britain' No. 34067 *Tangmere*, in charge of 'The Cathedrals Express', was beyond my expectations. The train arrived just after 9.00 am, at which time I initially met the locomotive's previous owner and now operations agent - John Bunch: due thanks were expressed for permitting this pre-arranged trip down to Salisbury.

The driver on the day was my old Nine Elms colleague and long-time friend, Peter Roberts. A brief exchange with his fireman, John Gibbins and another footplate guest was completed before we were soon signalled out on to the Down Through, followed shortly by the tip to depart from the guard. We were away. A steady, sure-footed start saw the train clear of the points before the serious work commenced, entering St John's cutting and the gradient ahead. Years before the 1906 introduction of the electro-pneumatic equipment that worked both lower quadrant gantry signals and points on the line, two intermediate signal boxes lay between Woking and Brookwood, namely 'St Johns' and 'Hermitage', the bases of these still discernible all these years later. Brookwood was also the former junction to the Necropolis Railway that served the two internal North and South stations in the huge cemetery on the down side. On the up side there was another junction that not only went to Bisley, the home of the National Rifle Association, but further on to a substantial military railway establishment at Deepcut.

Our original Bulleid light pacific was responding well to the Nine Elms touch that Peter has professionally retained over many years. Indeed it was an absolute pleasure to listen to, and observe once again, the varying aspects of the locomotive's progress, like the exhaust events in conjunction with the use of the regulator and cut-off position. At the same time the rather smokey coal on the tender was being deftly applied to the firebox by John Gibbins, certainly providing more than adequate pressure on occasions!

Beyond Pirbright Junction and with a load of eleven

Jim Lester, left, reviving old memories. As mentioned by him in the text, his autobiography, SOUTHERN REGION ENGINEMAN is still available, just, with less than 100 copies remaining in print.

This page - Comparisons. The top view is similar to, but not identical to that which appeared on the rear cover of SW12, and showing a tired and decrepit No. 34067 on the scrap line outside the rear of Eastleigh shed following withdrawal in late 1963. Ironically the LMR 8F ahead of it had arrived for, and was indeed received, repairs at the works. No 34067 though was towed off to the scarp yard at Barry from where it subsequently rescued and painstakingly restored to the condition seen below.

Opposite - No. 34007 'Wadebridge' leaving Whitchurch North with an up stopping train. The DNS line ran at 90 ° north - south under the LSWR between the footbridge and distant road overbridge. The DNS route closed to passengers in 1960 and all traffic in 1964.

P H Groom

coaches behind, speed was increasing all the time, more so after milepost 31 was passed. Remarkable to reflect that this locomotive was originally withdrawn from service in 1966, yet today handled the train with comparative ease, certainly a testimony to the long dedicated restoration programme and all the stalwarts that were, and indeed still are, involved. Standing on the tender plate, observing the mainline footplate activity, I quietly reflected on the many occasions that I had experienced such times previously: even so, today was really as good as it comes.

Through the narrow single-bore tunnel of the aqueduct carrying the Basingstoke canal above the line, this was immediately followed by the former Sturt Lane Junction, where from the local line it was originally possible to cross three other sets of rails and peel off to the right to Frimley Junction and thence on to Ascot. Today we continued over the now single Ash Vale line and then what little is left of the old trailing junction that came off the Frimley route.

Really into our stride now, Farnborough was passed with ever increasing speed, followed by the long-gone Bramshot Halt and then on to Fleet. In the past this was where the compressed air was produced and stored for the line's electro-pneumatic operation. In later years serious consideration was given to the provision of water troughs in several locations, one of them being between Farnborough and Fleet. After in depth examination the scheme was eventually abandoned.

Winchfield, then Hook were both soon in our wake. Then, when coming out of the deep cutting after Hook, we passed the remnants of the little siding at Newnham, always a location question that you were asked when discussing your route knowledge back at Nine Elms in the fifties and sixties. Incidentally, at Hook it had been the practice to test the water tap on a Bulleid tender, located immediately behind the driver, a good indicator to the amount of water that was left. No water appearing from the tap was not a good omen and an out-of-course water stop at Basingstoke was not unknown in some such circumstances, more so when working down the Salisbury road.

We had no concerns about water today as we thundered through Basingstoke at speed with green signals ahead on up towards what were the old semaphore intermediate block signals at Winklebury followed by Worting Junction. In the process we passed what looked like the yard shunting neck on the left: in fact is the last remnant of the original track-bed of the line to Alton, made famous by Will Hay in the film 'Oh Mr. Porter'!

At Battledown, originally a flat junction, we branched away right under the flyover now carrying the original London & Southampton Railway up line, and made our way west on the much later built L&SWR line. The small village of Oakley had earlier had a station, sadly gone since 1963; however an overbridge still retained its white painted brickwork that aided observation of the semaphore 'Home' signal on its approach. Overton is next and the large works located there is seen in advance of the approach to the station. Situated on the up side, it was known as the 'Pound Note Factory' to many footplate crews due to its production of highly-specialised paper and bank notes.

On further to the former three-platform station, Whitchurch North, as it was called in BR steam days, due to there being two stations here. The other was just down below the end of the platform in the valley on the left. This was on the former GWR line, originally known as the DNS (Didcot, Newbury & Southampton), a line built by that company quite late, in 1885, purely intended to tap into the docks and through traffic to the Midlands and beyond. Now down through Hurstbourne and across the viaduct and the watercress beds that lie below. Rumour had it that certain Nine Elms drivers had actually set fire to the same cress beds below, such was the manner that they worked their locomotives.

Climbing now, past the location of Hurstbourne Junction that once took trains to Longparish, Wherwell and on to Fullerton Junction and the Test valley line. Onward up to the top of the bank, beyond which the area is known as Enham. During the three mile 1 in 178 downward sweep in semaphore days, the fireman would be looking for the down distant for Andover Junction: essential to catch this one early for the driver, as speed was usually quite high. Indeed today we were doing very well ourselves

Once the flyers on the West of England trains, but by 1957 eking out their remaining years on more mundane workings. 'T9' No. 30729 with a local goods working at Andover in 1957.

and Peter reduced the steam chest pressure as our speed hovered around 75mph. Clearly *'Tangmere'* wanted to go faster, like many of its class mates had before, but sadly some restraint was necessary. Never mind, it was still a fantastic feeling as we approached the station at high speed and with a lingering blast on the whistle were through the platform and were instantly climbing again, 1 in 220 up to Red Post Junction, where the old Midland & South Western Junction Railway line branched away to our right on its original route to Cheltenham. Looking back, I recall one morning working down with the 9.00am Waterloo - Salisbury – Exeter, and when running into Andover Junction, there was an engine sticking out through the demolished back wall of the small engine shed. I daresay her driver booked her requiring new brake blocks that day..... .

With the immediate ascent of the bank up to Grateley the regulator position was again supplying the steam chest, valves and cylinders with ample pressure. Years earlier, beyond the signals at Red Post Junction, there was a further intermediate block signal at Monxton that broke up the rather long climbing section. The almost seven mile ascent eventually eased at milepost 71¼ when passing under a large girder bridge just west of Grateley.

A single line from Grateley to Amesbury and Bulford Camp was built in 1904 and ran parallel alongside the Up road

for two and a quarter miles before finally disappearing into the distance over Salisbury Plain towards Stonehenge. There had been a triangular track layout that also allowed traffic from Salisbury direct access to the Amesbury branch. Such was the movement of military equipment in and out of the large army camp at Bulford that it actually warranted a flying junction to be built, appropriately known as Amesbury Junction. Later when the line was eventually abandoned and the track lifted it was renamed Allington and the controlling signal box was left to act as an intermediate box. The top-secret military research establishment on Porton Down is actually skirted by the railway line and Idmiston Halt, taking its name after a nearby village, was eventually built for the civilian employees. This was followed by Porton station, about a quarter of a mile further west after passing through the deep chalk cutting around the corner. Both these stopping places have been disused since 1968. We hastened through what little was left to observe of the original station, then on down through the Winterbournes, descending at 1 in 169 and on to a really fast bit of the line indeed. Another interesting rumour had it that a certain driver on sighting a red light in the far distance one dark night attempted to stop at it, embarrassingly only to find out it was actually the one located on the top of the spire of Salisbury Cathedral down in the valley.

Displaying the headcode for a Portsmouth service, another 'T9', this one No. 30289 , on the turntable at Salisbury LSW shed, 3 October 1953.

During the drop down towards Tunnel Junction the finishing touches would have been made to the normally quite substantial fire in a Bulleid pacific, particularly a 'Merchant Navy', ready for the relieving crew. Many of the rather dour but senior Exmouth Junction firemen were aged in their late forties in those days, but certainly seemed to cheer up somewhat when they saw the huge fire rolling out of the fire-hole door.

Today we were running quite early and with previous caution signals we steadily approached Tunnel Junction and stopped on the triangle of lines. Strange, but ironic in many ways, was the installation of the Laverstock loop on what was just an embankment all those years ago. It was in fact part of the original 1857 built route from Basingstoke to Salisbury's Milford terminus, the city's very first station. The departure of a Portsmouth service finally cleared our path into Salisbury's platform 4 and we entered the platform where a crowd of people awaited.

My footplate trip was over all too soon as we arrived at Salisbury, where we had quite some dwell time. So, once stationary, I went back with Peter to the support coach whilst some of the support team serviced the locomotive. It was when chatting with the rest of the team that John Bunch asked me if I'd like to continue through to Honiton. Well, what can you say to an offer like that?

Previously I had never ridden on the footplate over this section of the line, indeed it had been an ambition never previously achieved, and one that I believed was long, long gone. Many were the times that I had watched our relieving crew at Salisbury restarting the train from London, bound for the West of England and had wondered just what it would be like to work over the route? Well, I was about to find out all these years later and on rejoining the footplate I found John busily building up the fire for the journey ahead.

Peter in the meantime made some last minute enquiries before returning to the cab where he then ensured all was well on the footplate before making ready for departure. In next to no

time we were away and as we passed the sad remains of Salisbury's loco shed heading up to Wilton South, I must say that I was really looking forward with anticipation to the next train of events: I was not to be disappointed.

It was evident Peter knew the route particularly well and 'Tangmere' was really put through her paces as we accelerated up the initial 1 in 115 gradient. Today's track layout is in stark contrast to that of yesteryear, single line sections with passing loops all controlled by colour light signals, as one would expect. The former separate Southern and Great Western stations at Wilton are also now a distant memory to those that can recall such times.

Years earlier in 1947, Nine Elms men had learned the road through to Wilton South ready for the post-war introduction of the 'Devon Belle', an all-Pullman express complete with Observation Car. The idea was that the locomotive change would not take place at Salisbury, but out of sight around the corner.

Despite some dips in the profile of the line, the gradient is, in the main, much against us until Semley, where the summit is reached. However the dip at Wilton, milepost 85¼, certainly allowed 'Tangmere' to gain some extra speed as we passed Ditchampton School, then crossed the River Wylie and continued along the Nadder Valley. Between Dinton and Semley the line is a series of successive curves and the few dips that do exist aided our progress. Tisbury, still an operational single platform station, was passed with a longer than usual use of the whistle - as requested for someone's mum who lives nearby. As we neared the top of the climb we passed milepost 100, quite an ascent and once over the crest of the bank Peter took advantage to reset both the regulator and cut-off position on the initial falling gradient of 1 in 100 that continues for a good four miles until Gillingham.

I had been watching with interest Peter's method in using the steam reverser, identical to the manner that many former Nine Elms men applied. Always there was a reduction in steam chest pressure before attempting to notch up. Having achieved the setting required, the regulator was reset once again! Why? Well, steam reversers sometimes have a mind of their own: indeed, they could inexplicably drop into full forward gear or even reverse on occasions. This simple reduction in steam chest pressure initially assisted the reverser's movement of the valves and in the event of a mishap, saved the fire being lifted by a sudden blast and literally going up the chimney: it also reduced the shock of such an action and indeed averted the outside chance of a boiler surge causing priming. There was also a reduction of the dire consequences of an engine being suddenly thrust into reverse with a large regulator opening. Another little point that Peter and I discussed, was that many of the enginemen that we fired to in the past carried a bit of chalk in their pockets and would mark the sector plate and pointer for ease of observation, in both day and night.

Caution signals approaching Gillingham saw the train speed reduced accordingly and we ran steadily into the Dorset station. During our fine run from Salisbury a red fault light was noted on the On Train Monitoring Recorder (OTMR) equipment, now carried on the footplate of all mainline steam locomotives. As such this was duly reported and was immediately investigated by John Bunch. One of the tender cupboards now houses the electronics that provide the power for the statutory Driver Monitoring/Recording device that can be downloaded in the event of an incident. John went through the whole system and when he was satisfied, reset and re-tested the OTMR successfully. He concluded that a serious jolt en route was the likely cause of the failure. Indeed no further problems were observed.

The reasonable gradient at the initial start from Gillingham soon turns into something quite arduous, and the climb, 1 in 100 up, to Buckhorn Weston tunnel (742 yards) and the summit just beyond is made all the harder from a dead stand. Compare this with fast trains that could attack the bottom of the incline at 80 mph plus and lose but 20 mph on the full ascent.

On the footplate, extreme care is essential when entering tunnels. There is always the inherent danger of a blowback through an open fire-hole door. When necessary, drivers would indicate to their preoccupied fireman when a tunnel was being approached, particularly at night. Any attention to the fire would cease immediately and the fire door would be closed and the blower applied. The main cause of such an event is the close proximity between some tunnels roofs and the locomotive's chimney. This situation has been compounded over many years by the increased size of locomotives , including boiler dimensions that have finally reached the maximum loading gauge limit.

Then add to this the possibility of another train entering the tunnel at the same time, the combined effect literally further compressing the air in the confined space. This could be catastrophic if the previous precautions were not always rigidly applied. Another tunnel danger was that of slipping due to a damp interior, in particular where the gradient is still against you and the regulator is still well open. Under these circumstances the driver must be ready to react immediately at the first hint of a slip, indeed use of the steam sanding gear before entry is a wise precaution.

Once our train was clear of Buckhorn Weston tunnel, milepost 107½ the top of the bank is attained and the gradient reverses, inasmuch that the immediate downgrade is now simi-larly 1 in 100 and speed soon picks up, so by the time the bottom of the bank is reached at milepost 110, we were back well on the 70 mph plus mark. After this the gradient levels out for one mile, the respite is short though and immediately we are back against the collar as the gradient seesaws back to 1 in 80 on the severe approach up to Templecombe. However our progress does not last for too long as a Distant colour-light checks our speed in order to leave the single line section and join the double track again after Templecombe station. A steady approach towards the Stop signal sees the time-delay-operated signal clear to Green in good time and steam was immediately re-applied to regain the lost momentum on the rising gradient.

The years have not been too kind to many of the stations on this magnificent line, none more so than to Templecombe. This once vibrant little junction station was indeed unusual, certainly in the manner that it connected with the trains from Bath and Bournemouth that crossed beneath its path on the former Somerset & Dorset line. Little actually remains to remind those of us that spent perhaps too short a time, standing on its interchange platform and who witnessed the unique passenger train shunting manoeuvres in this quiet rural corner of Somerset. Even its small engine shed, set on the edge of the rolling countryside, oddly hosted locomotives from the Midlands that normally would have been more at home in the peaks of Derbyshire. How could anyone ever forget a railway whose character was so very special? Its closure at the time dealt a massive blow to the local community, likened to the many devastating coal-mining pit closures during the 'eighties and the similar effect on their own rural communities.

Such melancholy thoughts were fleeting as we passed through the sole existing platform, rejoined the double track section, and continued tackling the now slightly-eased gradient for the next two miles. Once clear of the summit, the long disused Milborne Port station was passed which then heralded the commencement of a six-mile fast section of the line, down through the ancient town of Sherborne and beyond, quite a lengthy stretch of it being 1 in 80. Like the earlier approach to old Andover Junction, the Sherborne experience was just as spectacular, the long blast on the whistle indicated that steam was back in the West of England and warned all God-Fearing Men of our fast approach, even so speed was yet again duly reined in to meet the current regulations.

With the gradient now in our favour, we continued running at high speed for another two miles before the next adverse change in the gradient profile. Nothing as extreme as previously encountered, this was a mere 1 in 250 for about a mile, before dropping down on the approach to Yeovil Junction. The alignment of the original Salisbury & Yeovil Railway (S&YR) to its original terminus in Yeovil, dating back to 1860, swings away to the right just before we pass over the former GWR line to Weymouth. The S&YR was eventually absorbed into the L&SWR in 1878, giving the latter company sole operating rights over the complete route to Exeter. Despite the decline in the fortunes of the route since the mid-1960s, as a station Yeovil Junction has fared the best of all considering the draconian cuts that took place. Indeed, it still retains its historical railway ambience that is sadly lost in other locations. The original downside platforms now provide the headquarters for the South West Main Line

No. 30451 'Sir Lamorak' with Urie tender, near Gillingham on 19 April 1958. The train would appear to consist of at least six horse-boxes, probably running empty.

Steam Centre that maintains the station buildings and some track which also includes the original turntable.

In my recent book 'Southern Region Engineman', I have devoted a section to the introduction in 1937 of R. E. L. Maunsell's Class V ('Schools') on the route as far as Yeovil Junction. Here they were turned and serviced before their return to Waterloo. In August 1962 due to the failure of the booked 'Merchant Navy' hauling the up 'Atlantic Coast Express', No. 30934 *St Lawrence,* conveniently in the yard at Yeovil Junction the time, was initially called upon to work the complete 'ACE' forward to Salisbury after which it actually continued on to Waterloo. What an incredible event, I know as I was the fireman on the footplate from Salisbury.

As we made our way into Yeovil Junction's former Up line platform, the branch line from Yeovil Town came in from our right. Previously this line was served by a regular service known locally as the 'The Bunk' and, like many other branch lines off the main line, motive power was a Drummond 'M7' and a 'Push & Pull' set: sadly there is no service connection today, just the tracks.

The station waiting time provided an opportunity to take photographs and the chance to observe the splendidly preserved original downside platform and the site of the former GWR station at Clifton Maybank. The turntable and pit are located at the end of the platform and will be used later today to provide the servicing facilities No. 34067 will use before the later return to London.

Eventually an incoming service off of the single line clears the way ahead and allows us to proceed to Honiton, our next scheduled stop. The route west continues in much the same fashion as we previously encountered from Salisbury. At milepost 123 we are sitting at the bottom of the bank that will eventually take us up past the old Sutton Bingham station to the summit at Kit Hill, the ruling gradient being 1 in 140 / 150 so there is a determined and early effort by Peter to accelerate our train away. I must say the engine has been working exceedingly well throughout the journey and continues to do so.

Once over the crest of the bank, the line thereafter descends into yet another valley and associated river, this time the River Parrett. Down now at 1 in 120 where the speed is increased in order to meet the challenge of the next bank. During occasions when permanent way repairs were necessary, a temporary speed restriction of 20mph or less at the foot of an incline could have quite a demanding effect on the footplate, particularly for the fireman, dependent that is on the prevailing gradient. The additional physical work that was generated by such events was quite substantial when the locomotive was further extended in an attempt to claw back the lost time. Certainly the severity of banks in the West of England that I had witnessed would require substantial effort from the crews involved. Indeed from milepost 130½ a gradient of 1 in 80 is met that continues through Crewkerne until the summit is reached some three miles later at milepost 133½.

Back in April 1953, 'Merchant Navy', No. 35020 *Bibby Line* survived a catastrophic crank axle failure here that subsequently resulted in the complete class of thirty engines being withdrawn from service. The fact that no one was killed or even injured is absolutely incredible, almost unbelievable, when one considers the magnitude of the mechanical failure on the day. Interesting times then ensued, as locomotives were borrowed from other regions of British Railways to substitute for the loss of the Southern's premier express type.

On the ascent of the bank between the hills of Shave and Curriot, yet another subterranean line feature is encountered, this is Hewish Tunnel at 209 yards. On then westward and plunging down into the Axe Valley we systematically criss-cross the River Axe on the thirteen-odd miles descent towards Axminster itself, taking us in and out of the shires of both Dorset and Somerset, finally crossing the Blackwater River before entering Devonshire, the county of our ultimate destination. Here restraint was again the order of the day and the speed of No. 34067 was reined in yet again. I recall one day in 1959 when as a passenger, and having just returned from Lyme Regis, I witnessed the extremely fast approach and passing of the 'ACE' whilst standing on Axminster station. Only then could I imagine just what the footplate experience was like on that day. Today I would almost find out for myself and I eagerly awaited our own approach and passing through. But before this we still had some ground to cover and were fast approaching old Chard Junction, now equally devoid of any signs of its former railway history, although once a centre for milk traffic and its link to the GWR at Chard itself. This is an extremely fast part of the line and in steam days speed would invariably have been well in excess of 85 mph for quite a sustained period of time, particularly on a non-stop service such as the 'ACE'. The falling gradient from Hewish Tunnel clearly allows the locomotive to be worked extremely economically in terms of valve setting and regulator position. Even out permitted present day maximum of 75 mph still provides a great sensation on the footplate. At last under clear signals we approach Axminster with the gradient subtly changing further in our favour from 1 in 255 to 1 in 240, there being only a brief chance to glimpse the sight of the Sir William Tite's station building, one of many on this stretch of the route.

Sadly Axminster station today is not unlike some of its counterparts on the route, now just single line, but at least still an operational station, albeit little else. We can but mentally reflect upon the past and yet still identify certain features that exist to this day reminding us of its former junction status. Remnants of the lightly laid, curvaceous little branch line to Lyme Regis that was indeed so special, as indeed were the Adams 0415 class 4-4-2T locomotives that plied the route for many years. The bay platform, located on the up side, still remains, though devoid of track and overgrown, bearing testimony to the service that it once provided to the seaside resort. From the bay the branch started with a short climb west before swinging south over the top of the main line then disappearing into the rolling hillside towards Combpyne and the Dorset Jurassic coast of Lyme Bay.

In the meantime we were fast approaching the bottom of the bank after which the working of the engine would change dramatically. The fireman on the trip, John, been positively active during the latter stages of our descent from Hewish Tunnel

in building up the depth of fire and filling the back corners of the 38.25 sq/ft firebox in readiness for the start of the climb of Honiton bank. Initially the climb starts at mile post 146¼, where an adverse gradient of 1 in 100 is first met, then up past Whitford, where the speed of our train gives us the momentum to tackle this early stage of the climb with relative ease. The fire immediately responded to the much heavier working of the engine and both the boiler pressure and water-level were ideal for what actually turned out to be a memorable ascent of this formidable bank.

Approaching the site of old Seaton Junction, the line almost levels out through the station area. Much remains here of typical Southern Railway style including the actual platforms. Much of the infrastructure consists of products of the Exmouth Junction concrete works. The original four main line tracks through here, now alas truncated to just a single line, permitted the overtaking of slow workings by faster trains. A modest, but healthy goods yard on the up side also provided sidings for local goods and milk traffic. Additionally there was the branch to Seaton and its two intermediate stations Colyton and Colyford. This line curved south, trailing away behind the signal-box on the down side.

The level short section of the line would normally have assisted us before the assault of the bank, however today it did not, for we had a 20mph Temporary Speed Restriction to contend with just beyond the defunct station and right at the bottom of the 1 in 80 incline. Accordingly speed was suitably reduced and it seemed an age before the complete train was past the restriction. Although I had experienced similar situations before, this provided the impetus for something rather special on the assault of Honiton bank.

Once the whole train was clear, Peter set the chain-driven valve-gear at 60% cut-off and fully opened the regulator. Soon both the steam chest pressure gauge and the boiler pressure gauge registered the same amount, 240 lbs p.s.i. and *'Tangmere'* instantly responded by attacking the bank. The weather was perfect, as was the railhead condition, as we began to accelerate from 20mph. The exhaust noise was phenomenal on the footplate: as, so a friend told me later, it was in the train. Indeed any line side observers were treated to a spectacle of Southern excellence as we dynamically forged our way westward. At that moment I thought that this was surely on a par with the mighty efforts of Swain and Hooker with No. 34004 *Yeovi* during the Exchange Trials.

What incredible engines they really were when in fine fettle and under the control of a masterly crew like today. I know that both my old friends Alan Wilton, a devotee of Bulleid's original locomotives, and indeed Bert Hooker would have derived great pleasure from this tremendous performance. Back in 1965 my own participation on the footplate of 'Battle of Britain' No. 34051 *'Winston Churchill'* during the railway funeral arrangements was a very special moment for me. Whilst the 'light' pacifics were fine performers it really was the larger 8P 'Merchant Navy' class that were the true masters of this route, in the right enginemen's hands - with their extra power, they could certainly handle the heaviest of the expresses of the day.

When talking to two senior retired Salisbury enginemen recently, a story concerning the 'ACE' was related. It involved an original Merchant Navy during an extremely fast run down to

Sidmouth Junction. On arrival a smartly-suited gentleman emerged from the train with clipboard in hand and approached the cab. He politely asked the driver "What was the speed of the train through Axminster?" The driver innocently declared "85mph". "Are you sure?" was the incredulous response. Again the driver curtly replied "85mph", this being the official line speed. "Well," said the unruffled gentleman ,"Actually I timed you at exactly 112 mph." I am sure there are many more similar tales that could be told about this legendary express.

Joining the railway service when I did in late 1957 did not allow me the opportunity of main line working on any of the original 'Merchant Navy' class locomotives. However I did record several occasions of preparation and disposal duties and some minor movements in the London area with those that still remained. All would be destined to receive British Railway's modification program that would be concluded in 1959.

On the original design, the fireman had to contend with a cab that was hot to work in and disposal was an extremely arduous task, principally as I recall, allotted to junior men. This required the 48.5 sq/ft firebox's accumulation of clinker and ash

'Push & Pull' fitted 'M7', No. 30021, seen waiting for departure time at Seaton Junction. Note the painted duty number 606 on the head-code disk rather than the pasted variety, no doubt due to the regular workings over the branch and the period the engine remained at the 72A's sub-depot shed.

(and there was plenty of it on occasions) to be thrown out by shovel rather than being dropped through a rocking grate, quite a strenuous operation. I had muscles in those days that even Charles Atlas would have been proud to possess. Rebuilding in the late `fifties did eventually rectify this particular downside, and whilst they remained an admirable engine in their new guise they were never ever the same again.

Notwithstanding these issues the original engines were very special, as the enginemen from the depots of Nine Elms, Salisbury and Exmouth Junction would wholly testify. In fact all the performances over this particular road and indeed on routes west of Exeter on to the Withered Arm were duly recognized by the Exmouth Junction enginemen in a testimonial presented to O. V. S. Bulleid in 1967. A true mark of appreciation from the West of England footplate crews for the former Southern Railway's CME's mainline locomotives.

Back on the footplate of No. 34067, the climb to the summit was outstanding, past the site of Honiton Incline signal-box that in semaphore days broke up the long section between Seaton Junction and Honiton and kept trains on the move. Speed was a creditable 40mph plus when we entered the 1,353yd tunnel, at which point the gradient had eased slightly although still climbing at 1 in 132. Again great care was applied throughout and a small slip, due to the wet interior, was immediately rectified without a problem. We crested the top of the bank inside the tunnel and with the falling gradient of 1 in 90 now very much in our favour, emerged from the tunnel's west portal.

Now gathering speed all the time on the long curve, Peter eased 'Tangmere' right back, as soon we would be approaching Honiton station where my footplate journey would end. During the stand-over time I made my way back to the support coach once more for a welcome cup of tea and where I also attempted to

wash off the grime of the day.

In years gone by, a bucket of hot water on the footplate would have been drawn off in good time in order to cool before use, with a couple of tool-box spanners inserted that stopped water spilling everywhere. Whilst the driver washed up, you would take his seat and observe the road ahead, then it was your turn to carry out your own ablutions. Naturally by this time, firing would have ceased sometime previously, the fire being suitably run down for the end of the journey and the final return to the shed for disposal.

What a truly amazing experience it had turned out to be - one that evoked such strong, vivid memories from the early 1960s. I wondered how many other old colleagues would have changed places with me in my privileged position today: I suspect far too many to name, for sure.

The demise and end of steam I know affected a lot of like-minded loco-men and the emergence of the first preserved railways did not immediately appeal to many colleagues. But as time passed they actually became the saviours of many a representative of a class of locomotive that were scheduled to be cut-up and thereby lost forever. A number of years ago, when on a visit to the Mid-Hants Railway, I clearly remember seeing a decrepit 'Battle of Britain', in a deplorable state after its withdrawal. Actually it was the same No. 34067, *Tangmere*. Who would ever have thought today would have been possible - certainly not me!

On behalf of the many retired Southern Enginemen of those times may I sincerely thank each and every one that has ever been involved in these restoration projects, we are indeed grateful beyond that which words can say.

Happier times for the final member of the class, Bricklayers Arms based No. 30939 'Leatherhead' seen on a Kent Coast working.

Left - *In February 1962, to the fitting accompaniment of snow flurries, the end is nigh for No. 30900 Eton, the first of the Schools Class, at one time the candidate for preservation as representative of the type, but which was unceremoniously scrapped at Ashford Works the following month.*

FROM PUBLIC SCHOOL TO BORSTAL

Jeffery Grayer recalls the transfer of no less than 16 members of the Schools Class to Brighton between 1959 and 1962, to complement the two examples based here from 1958. He also examines the latter-day history of the doyen of the Schools Class, No. 30900 'Eton', which was at one time a candidate for preservation, but which ended its career ignominiously dumped at Brighton shed for over a year before being ultimately scrapped at Ashford Works.

Although several members of the 'Schools' Class had enjoyed brief sojourns based at Brighton before the late 1950s, these being No. 30915 (27/3/53 – 26/5/53), No. 30922 (8/10/51-30/6/52), Nos. 30928 and 30929 (11/46-10/47) and No. 30930 (11/46-12/47), we take up the story in the summer of 1958 when the first of what was to become a positive deluge of these machines descended upon 75A. With the introduction of Stage II of the Hastings Line Diesel Scheme in June 1958, St Leonard's depot consequently closed losing its steam allocation which at the time included three of Maunsell's 'Schools' Class. No. 30902 was transferred to Nine Elms but Nos. 30900 and 30901 found their way to Brighton shed. Here they were put to work on the many Summer Saturday inter-regional trains which in those days also warranted the operation of many reliefs to cope with demand. Their appearance on these services was not without incident however, when for example No. 30900 stopped on the 1 in 53 incline of North Pole bank on the 9 August with a 10 coach inter-regional service from Brighton, which it was powering as far as Willesden, and was unable to restart having to be rescued by WC Class No. 34047 *Callington*. Also on that day L Class No. 31777 was stopped on the same bank but managed to restart its train. With two of 75A's Pacifics incarcerated in Eastleigh Works for modification, No. 34045 (29/7-17/10) and No. 34047 (10/9-1/11), increasing use was made of 'Schools' on the depots principal top link duties during this period. In addition to Nos. 30900/01, both No. 30936 and No. 30909 appeared on workings from Brighton in September 1958.

Early in the New Year the reliability of No. 30900 was again called into question when on 13 February 1959 the 05:32 van train from London Bridge to Brighton required the attachment of No. 30901, reportedly at Three Bridges, ahead of an ailing No. 30900, the pair managing a respectable, in the circumstances, 15 minute late arrival into Brighton. Newhaven boat trains were generally steam hauled by Pacifics at this time although reliefs saw 'Schools' in action including Nos. 30900/1/8/9/15/37 at Easter 1959. Nos. 30914/5, which arrived to swell the 'Schools' numbers at 75A in June, found themselves being used in turn with Nos. 30900/1 on weekday through trains to Bournemouth. Saturday inter-regional traffic continued to be worked by 'Schools', helped out by U1 moguls, generally running to and from Willesden although on 25 July no less than six members of the K class were noted in action on these services.

With the arrival of Nos. 30916/7 in July 1959, Brighton had an allocation of no less than five Pacifics and six 'Schools' with which to work just four top link duties, reducing to only three in winter. However, the long term bugbear of 75A, low maintenance performance, continued to haunt the depot with standards at a lower ebb than ever, meaning locomotives were out of service for long periods or were unreliable once in traffic. For example on the 8 October no Pacific could be found for duty No.733 so No. 30916 was rostered even though 'Schools' were prohibited over a certain portion of the route covered by this duty. No. 30916 duly double headed the 23:18 mails to London Bridge and returned with the 03:27 thence to Eastbourne. No. 30916 then took on 10:03 Eastbourne – Brighton but subsequently failed. It is not known whether this locomotive operated the 08:16 Eastbourne – Hailsham part of this duty, but if it did then it shouldn't have done as the class was banned from the Hailsham route! No. 30915 appeared on the Saturday 13:55 Brighton – Victoria service at this time in place of the more usual Stewarts Lane N mogul.

On 12 January 1960 *Eton* worked the 07:19 Brighton – London Bridge and return at 16:40, also working the 18:10 from Victoria on 4 and 6 February. Despite its somewhat rundown external appearance it reportedly gave a very good performance on both evenings so the overhaul it had just received at Ashford Works must have been beneficial. On 14 January No. 30917 worked the 17:37 London Bridge – East Grinstead for the first time and after turning on the triangle at East Grinstead returned with the 19:26 to Victoria. 'Schools' also turned their hand to freight work on the Central Section with No. 30917 deputising for a K mogul on the 22:30 Hove – Norwood returning with the 03:40 the following morning. No. 30901 worked the 21:32 Brighton to Norwood on another occasion and No. 30914 was spotted on the 13:05 Norwood – Lewes goods.

In May 1960, three Brighton based 'Schools' were sent to Redhill for use on Reading line and they were replaced by Standards Nos. 76053-5 from Redhill. In the event Brighton could not get on with these Standards so they were in turn replaced by Nine Elms 'Schools' Nos. 30902/18/19 and by 8 May Nos. 30902 and 30919 had both appeared on the Brighton to Bournemouth run. The bulk of the summer inter-regional services in 1960 were handled not by K moguls as previously but by the ever increasing ranks of supernumerary 'Schools' and U1s. On 7 September 1960 passengers on the 06:22 Seaford to Brighton electric service were treated to steam haulage for part of the way after their 2-BIL unit failed at Newhaven where, as luck would have it, none other than No. 30900 was waiting to run light to Polegate. It was therefore commandeered to assist the EMU to Lewes where the train was terminated. This may well represent the last reported sighting of No. 30900 in action. Shortly after No. 30900 was noted in Ashford Works with a badly corroded cab and supports where it received a further light casual overhaul. In early October 1960 there were no fewer than eight 'Schools' in the shops, Nos. 30900/6/9/11/15/27/29/37 with 30905/10 expected shortly. The laying aside of No. 30909 in the yard, pending a decision on its future, looked at that time as if it was to be a likely candidate for the first 'Schools' withdrawal. Additionally by the year end, in spite of its recent overhaul, No. 30900 was reported as being stored unserviceable at Brighton shed in dilapidated condition and here it was to remain for over a year. The extra seasonal parcels traffic that Christmas from Brighton was mainly entrusted to 'Schools' haulage.

Early in 1961 surprisingly No. 30909 was temporarily reprieved due to a shortage of motive power for the summer service. An unusual duty was performed by Brighton based 'Schools' when they were employed to provide steam heat for a special train stationed at Hove. The locomotives involved were No. 30907 on 17 March and No. 30901 the following day. In connection with the BR Amateur Boxing competition, the semi-finals for which were held at Hove Town Hall on 17 March, a special train was provided to accommodate the contestants. It consisted of 4 LMR sleeping cars, 1 WR sleeping car, a SR restaurant car and a SR open second. Brighton 'Schools' wandered as far as the Redhill-Reading line as one of 75A's duties involved going forward from Redhill with 11:43 Wolverhampton train and working back with the 14:50 Reading-Redhill.

Following its dumping at Brighton No. 30900 was not to be formally withdrawn until January 1962 by which time nearly half of the class had already gone. It was initially hauled from Brighton to the deserted St Leonards shed on 24 September 1961 by N Class mogul No. 31832 pending a final decision upon preservation. The decision apparently made, the last two Vulcans (C2X) made their own farewell runs on 3 February 1962 when No. 32535, running light from Three Bridges, and No. 32523 from Brighton, coupled up at Lewes and proceeded to extract No. 30900 from St Leonards shed hauling it on its final journey to

Ashford. It was to be cut up here in w/e 17 March 1962, almost 32 years to the day after entering traffic.

The record card for No. 30900, held at the National Archives, has never been amended and still indicates that it had been preserved! Even before the first 'Schools' withdrawals came in January 1961, with Nos. 30919 and 30932, the British Transport Commission had already decided upon preserving an example of the class. In 1960 the BTC had added 27 locomotive types to the national preservation wish-list, 19 of which were suggested by a consultative panel and 8 by the BTC. No. 30900 was initially earmarked as the representative of the class. However the appearance of this first of the class had been radically altered by the addition of a Lemaitre exhaust, fitted in June 1940, and a large chimney whilst additionally the locomotive was not in particularly good condition during its final months. These were factors which doubtless caused it to be passed over for preservation in favour of an unmodified example, No. 30925 *Cheltenham*. Following withdrawal No. 30925 was sent to Fratton for storage and today can be seen at York Railway Museum.

Along with Nos. 30914/19/32, *Eton* was one of the few 'Schools' to go to the breakers in black livery, never having received green, nor did it have AWS fitted though it did receive a speedometer in January 1960. Whilst lying derelict at Brighton it had its nameplates removed and by June 1961 a scrawled inscription 'Borstal' had been substituted on the backing plate either by a disaffected railwayman or some enthusiast wag. For those who don't know, in the United Kingdom a borstal was a specific kind of youth prison, run by the Prison Service and intended to reform seriously delinquent young people. The word is sometimes used, incorrectly, to apply to other kinds of youth institution or reformatory, such as Approved Schools and Detention Centres. The court sentence was officially called "borstal training". Borstals were originally for offenders under 21, but in the 1930s the age was increased to under 23. The Criminal Justice Act of 1982 abolished the borstal system in the UK, introducing youth cus-

No. 30901 Winchester seen at Brighton shed in early 1962. Together with Eton this locomotive was transferred to Brighton from St Leonard's shed upon its closure in June 1958.

Nos. 30900 Eton leading No. 30901 Winchester in Brighton shed yard.

Rod Blencowe collection

tody centres instead. This state of affairs for a woebegone No. 30900 was indeed a far cry, not only from the grandeur of the public school name originally carried but from its pristine appearance upon its entry into traffic in March 1930 when it was proudly exhibited at Waterloo on 26 March and at Windsor & Eton Riverside station on 28-29 March where pupils from its namesake public school viewed the locomotive. No. 30900 was not the only school to be unofficially christened however, 30902 *Wellington* had the suffix 'Boot' scrawled in the dirt on its splasher and on its smoke deflectors in at least one published shot taken in October 1962 (Irwell Press *The Book of The Schools 4-4-0s*). However, as with many others of its Class the nameplate from 'Eton' was preserved and can now be seen displayed in the School of Mechanics within Eton College.

Until the end of 1961 Brighton based 'Schools' operated services from Victoria to Brighton via Tunbridge Wells West and less successfully the heavy 07:17 Brighton – London Bridge and 16:40 return on which they unfortunately developed a habit of stalling on Falmer Bank coming out of Lewes. As a result they were replaced by Bulleids from 4 December 1961. The through Wolverhampton train was restored for a few days around Christmas 1961 with No. 30911 evident on the Redhill - Brighton section. On 7 January 1962 a specially cleaned No. 30901 worked an enthusiasts' special from Eastleigh to Swindon works via Southampton and Westbury returning via Reading and Basingstoke, probably the first and last visit of a 'Schools' to Swindon. Although No. 30901 also worked the 0955 Victoria - Brighton on 3 March and on 5 March had charge of the 0624 Tonbridge – Brighton, in general 'Schools' were much less in evidence early in the New Year in this area than they had previously been. The reintroduction of the Brighton - Bournemouth through train saw Nos. 30901/17/28 in use in April. No. 30901 took the limelight again when, together with two K Class moguls, it was one of the standby engines for Royal Train duty on Derby Day. When No. 34013 *Okehampton* dropped a plug with the 11:30 Brighton – Plymouth on 26 June, No. 30923 came to the rescue at Shoreham-by-sea.

No. 30929 took on the heavy Glasgow car sleeper on 11 August as far as Willesden but in general 'Schools' were confined to occasional trips from their home depot. They were by now relatively infrequent performers on the Oxted line, No. 30901 making a feeble run on 26 October with the 1855 Brighton-Victoria, losing time all the way. Even as late as November 1962 Brighton based 'Schools' appeared spasmodically on through trains as far as Salisbury, the 1250 Cardiff – Brighton had 'Schools' haulage on three days in w/e 10 November. No. 30915, late of Redhill shed, was apparently in appalling external condition, suggestive of already long dereliction, but proved game to the last by taking on a Brighton - Salisbury working as one of its final duties. Of ten Pacifics on the strength at 75A only two were serviceable in early December necessitating No. 30916 stepping into the breach and hauling the 11:30 Plymouth service on both the 4 and 5 December.

The RCTS 'Sussex Special' of November with No. 30925 gave Sussex enthusiasts a last chance to see a 'Schools' at the head of an express with a timing of 60 minutes for the run down the main Brighton line (it actually took 64 minutes with 7 coaches, although 7 minutes were put down to delays). Withdrawals had continued steadily since 1961, however withdrawal of Nos. 30912/17/28 in November gave no hint of what was to come the following month when at a stroke the last remaining 17 members of the class were axed. By no means all of this last group were in operational condition for several had been languishing unserviceable at the back of various sheds for some time. This cull was generally seen as an accounting move implemented to reduce steam stocks prior to the replacement of the British Transport Commission by the British Railways Board at the beginning of 1963. A similar fate befell the ex-LBSCR K-Class moguls, a class which had survived virtually intact, with only two withdrawals the previous month, until December when the remainder of this 17 strong class were summarily despatched. In fact 63 locomotives were withdrawn by the Southern Region that month rendering Classes V, K, Z, E6, H16, 700 and 0298 extinct. One of the last sightings of a 'Schools' on the Central Division of the Southern Region was that of No. 30911 on the

07:27 Reading to London Bridge on 28 December, it then took over the 16:40 London Bridge – Brighton via Oxted service. The following day *Dover* was unceremoniously sent from Brighton shed to the temporary dumping ground at Hove Goods Yard which it shared in company with Nos. 30901, 30915 and 30923. Brighton became something of an 'Elephant's Graveyard' for the 'Schools' with no fewer than seven examples coming here to die, spending only a month or so on 75A's books before withdrawal, two at the end of 1961 and five at the end of 1962 (Appendix 1).

It was with a sense of shock that enthusiasts learnt of the scale of the December slaughter, tinged with regret that they would no longer be able to see these fine machines in action. My own memories of them include seeing No. 30917 *Ardingly* re-turning on the through Brighton train after school at Chichester, No. 30901 *Winchester* in steam on Brighton shed where I also remember No. 30900 languishing unserviceable at the side of the shed although I don't personally recall the 'Borstal' soubriquet which was probably soon erased. I next saw them further afield on the scrap lines at Eastleigh shed where I photographed No. 30934 *St Lawrence* in the summer of 1963 being held awaiting the final call. No. 30934 was in fact the last example to be steamed in BR service when, as late as 18 May 1963, it was lit up to haul a dead 700 Class from Basingstoke shed to Eastleigh. Thus ended the career of one of the most handsome 4-4-0s ever to grace the railways of this country and the sad story of "what might have been" for the doyen of the class *Eton*.

Appendix 1: 'Schools' Class allocated to Brighton (75A) 1958 - 1962		
30900	Period ending 6.6.58 Stored at Brighton shed 10/60 - 2/62	Withdrawn: 2/62
30901 #	6.6.58	12/62
30914	16.6.59 - 6.5.60 thence to Redhill	7/61
30915 * #	14.6.59 - 6.5.60 thence to Redhill. 19.11.62 returned to Brighton	12/62
30916 *	18.7.59 - 6.5.60 thence to Redhill. 17.12.62 returned to Brighton	12/62
30917	18.7.59	11/62
30902	6.5.60 - 24.11.60 thence to Nine Elms	12/62
30918	6.5.60 - 24.11.60 thence to Nine Elms	10/61
30919	6.5.60	2/61
30911 * #	24.11.60 - 4.1.62 thence to Redhill. 17.12.62 returned to Brighton	12/62
30907	24.11.60	9/61
30920	10.2.61	11/61
30922 *	9.11.61	11/61
30923 * #	9.11.61	12/62
30928	9.11.61	11/62
30929	4.1.62	12/62
30906 *	19.11.62	12/62
30930 *	4.12.61 - 1.2.62 thence to Redhill. 17.12.62 returned to Brighton	12/62
* Withdrawn shortly after arrival at Brighton.		
# Subsequently stored in Hove Goods Yard.		

Left - No. 30915 Brighton is seen at Ashford on 25 February 1962. From June 1959 until May 1960 and again from November 1962 until withdrawal the following month this locomotive was appropriately based at its namesake location – Brighton shed 75A. Here it appears in a seasonal snowstorm with only a chalked or painted on name-plate.

Opposite top left - In much better condition, also at Ashford on the same day, is 30926 Repton which after crossing the Atlantic for a number of years, was repatriated to these shores and can now be found on the North Yorkshire Moors Railway

Top right - *The end of the road for the former No. 30934 St Lawrence which spent its last weeks at Basingstoke. AWS with its associated battery box seen on the running plate, had been fitted as late as May 1962 and so gives credence to the belief that just a few months earlier there had been no intention to cull the whole class by the end of the same year. No. 30934 is recorded outside the rear of Eastleigh running shed having been withdrawn in December 1962 and subsequently stored in Basingstoke yard until moved to Eastleigh in May 1963. It remained basically intact until July 1963 and was reported as cut up at the nearby works w/c 3 August 1963.*
Bottom - *No. 30910 Merchant Taylors outside Newhaven Town shed on 13 April 1958. At the time a Ramsgate engine, this was another engine that transferred to the western section, in this case to Nine Elms, but was withdrawn in December 1961 and cut up just a few days into the New Year.*

ALLAN COBB
A PHOTOGRAPHIC TRIBUTE

Allan Cobb was born in 1882, destined to be the first of what would be three generations of railwaymen. Despite being the son of a Master at Uppingham he was educated at Shrewsbury and whether by choice or direction is known to have commenced what was a premium apprenticeship with the SECR at Ashford circa 1900. His subsequent career path would see him progress through the ranks with both the SECR and later the Southern Railway rising to the post of Locomotive Running Superintendent at Deepdene reporting directly to Bulleid in WW2. He would retire from here on 31 October 1944. Jeremy Cobb recalls his grandfather as saying Bulleid was a difficult man to work for and they did not get on.

It would be wonderful to be able to plot the career and experiences of Allan Cobb in detail over those 40 odd years, although apart from the occasional reference to a transfer, promotion and then of course retirement, all of which mainly appear in the *SOUTHERN RAILWAY MAGAZINE*, details of his work appear sparse - so far as written content is concerned.

Instead however, his grandson Jeremy Cobb has inherited a veritable treasure trove of photographic images, some official, some from news magazine, and the occasional snapshot, but covering various incidents and occasions on the SECR / SR and it is this then we must use to attempt to piece together a record of that life.

All three members of the Cobb dynasty held senior positions on the railway. Allan Cobb's son, Robert Cobb, joined the Southern as a 'Cadet' in 1936 rising to Stores Superintendent and subsequently Assistant General Manager, Technical and Commercial.

Jeremy Cobb was a management trainee on the Stoke Division of the LMR before career moved took him to Euston and then Birmingham as Customer Relations Manager. Jeremy Cobb would very much like to be able to fill in some of the gaps in the history of his grandfather and any contributions towards this would be welcome.

The first image we know of Allan Cobb, seen on the tender of 'D' class 4-4-0 No. 75. the occasion was no doubt riding experience

Above - Women carriage cleaners at London Bridge in 1918. The 'CR' does not, as has been mistaken in the past, stand for 'Caledonian Railway', but instead is one half of a sliding door vacuum cleaning unit, the door with the initial 'SE' being obscured.

Right - Self explanatory at Bricklayers Arms. The two views on this page are a clue perhaps to the career path of Allan Cobb, possibly already veering towards the operational rather than design side of the locomotive department. Here as later, the illustrations may well be indicative of occasions that held a specific significance in his career.

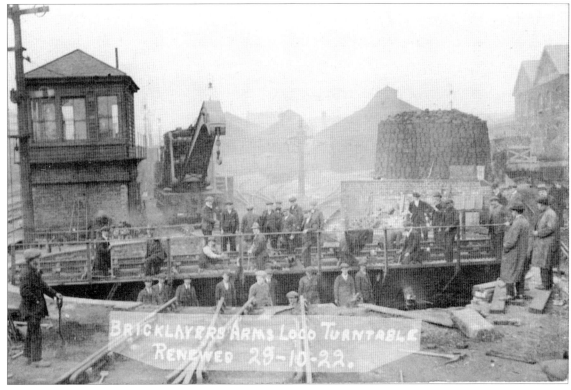

BRICKLAYERS ARMS LOCO TURNTABLE RENEWED 28-10-22.

Opposite page - *Press images of race day workings at Tattenham Corner, certainly post-WW1 but prior to the grouping. The abundance of horse boxes representing any number of the existing railway companies is worth a second look. Possibly these images were retained as he may have been involved in supervising what were prestige workings of the period. From a personal perspective we know that when he joined the SECR at Ashford he had taken digs in the town before moving around consequent upon his career path. He married circa 1915 and certainly post-1923 was living in the territory covered by the then Central Section travelling to London daily. Mr Jupp, a subsequent Footplate Inspector on the Southern Region who was then a fireman on the Brighton line, later recalled "...there was hell to pay if he was on the train and we were late." (Jeremy Cobb later recalled travelling with Mr Jupp when the latter as Inspector accompanied Jeremy on the footplate of the 'ACE' from Waterloo to Salisbury and return in Spring 1964.)*

Above - *One of the sadder occasions it was his responsibility to attend were a number of the accidents and incidents that occurred on the SR. None more so than that at Sevenoaks on 24 August 1927. Here Allan Cobb is seen walking towards the camera alongside the derailed last coach: a 1923 built 3rd brake, No. 3575. Much has been written of the causes of this accident: locomotive - v - permanent way, these will not be repeated here although this and subsequent images do afford a visual glimpse at the apparent conditions of the track and ballast which were commented upon in the subsequent accident report. * (Views of the damaged engine from this accident appear on pages 66/67 of Issue 7.)*

* A copy of the report can be seen at: http://www.railwaysarchive.co.uk/documents/MoT_Sevenoaks1927.pdf

Both pages - *The sad and tragic scene. Clearly the macabre held a ghoulish fascination for the onlookers. Seen are the Pullman Car 'Carmen' as well as two other vehicles, both according to the official accident report, 1925-built composites, Nos. 988 and 5533. The presence of the women on the trackside, opposite top, is slightly curious. Had they even been passengers? Sadly 13 persons died, 21 were seriously injured 40 slightly injured. A further 71 passengers complained of injury or shock the next day. Contemporary Press reports indicated there were 350 passengers in the train.*

This page - The Pullman car pulled clear of its position and ready for final removal. Whilst in no way wishing to trivialise what was the worst accident suffered by the Southern Railway, Allan Cobb's collection present what is probably the first time a succinct view of the tragedy has been presented.

Opposite top - Happier times. An unidentified Royal Train working behind a 'Lord Nelson'. No date is given but the reverse of the card gives a slight clue so far as the location is Fleet and the speed was reported as 85 mph. "Eleven members of the Royal Family were on board." The undated card also bears a note "From S & T Department, Guildford."

Opposite bottom - There were several presentations to Allan Cobb upon his retirement and likewise several dinners he would have attended in his formal capacity. One of the latter is shown here, on 11 December 1943 but without reference to the speech he was making at the time or indeed the occasion. Subsequent to his retirement, his former role of Locomotive Running Department was brought within the sphere of the Traffic Department, with the first post holder in the new role, T E Chrimes, taking the title Locomotive Running Superintendent. From a report in the Nov / Dec issue of the SR Magazine, we know that for part of his duties he had been involved with negotiating on staff matters and was indeed well respected for the way he had handled this aspect of his work. He was presented with an illuminated address by the men in recognition of this. Another presentation took place, this time on 15 February 1945, at a dinner at the Charing Cross Hotel. Here there were senior representatives from throughout the SR system, including such names as A B McLeod, H Holcroft and M S Hatchell. Aside from cheques and bouquets, "Mr Howard (Bricklayers Arms) presented Allan Cobb with a old pattern wooden bowl which Mr Cobb had used when he started on the SECR in 1900." Following his retirement, he moved to Hawkhurst.

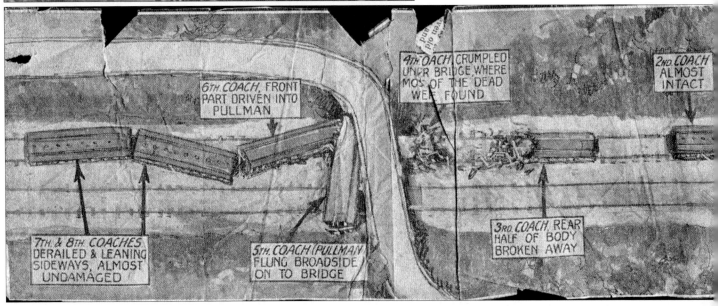

7TH. & 8TH. COACHES. DERAILED & LEANING SIDEWAYS, ALMOST UNDAMAGED

6TH. COACH. FRONT PART DRIVEN INTO PULLMAN

5TH. COACH (PULLMAN) FLUNG BROADSIDE ON TO BRIDGE

4TH. COACH CRUMPLED UNDER BRIDGE WHERE MOST OF THE DEAD WERE FOUND

2ND. COACH ALMOST INTACT

3RD. COACH. REAR HALF OF BODY BROKEN AWAY

STORIES FROM EAST GRINSTEAD TICKET OFFICE

Tom Henningsen

At East Grinstead the Ticket Office was combined with the Parcels Office and sported a small Ticket Office grill, Southern Railway style. The actual Ticket Office was connected to Parcels department via an open doorway (there was no actual door) whilst stable doors were provided to secure the area from the public. The office was staffed by an early and late turn booking clerks and a junior clerk, the latter mainly looking after parcels between 8.00 am and mid-day.

We had some specific traffic, some of which were medical people coming to the Queen Victoria Hospital where the plastic surgeon Sir Archibald McIndoe (1) trained staff from all over the country. Another notable was J A Dewar, the whiskey magnate, from whose stables mares would be sent to Eire. There were also greyhounds, sent throughout the country for stud.

"A problem with accents." A young lady arrives at the Ticket Office window and politely asks for a return "Tomorrow". Reply, "Where to?" - and again she repeated, "Tomorrow." This went on for some minutes or so and then I remember saying, "I appreciate you wish to return tomorrow but where are you going?" It was getting a little heated and the customer said "...tomorrow MURROW". We could find no fare in the fare book, but in the 1950s one could use the ABC timetable and add on the fare from London. That way we found it, and said, "You mean Murrow East…." The reply was, "Yes that right, to Morrow" - a station on the former M&GN line west of Wisbech. We had not understood purely because of her strong local accent. We would often enjoy the same joke with her in the future.

"It's a dog's life." In the morning rush hour Bill, the Railman in his sixties, pops his head to the window between the passengers. "Greyhound for the Dewar Estate." It was a hot day already and I replied I would telephone when the queue had died down. As an afterthought Bill said, "I have given the animal some water, loosened the collar, and tied it up on the grass in the yard - OK?"

I have no idea why, but after all passengers had cleared I decided to take a look at the animal's label before making the telephone call. What I found was no dog and instead just a collar and lead with the bitch rapidly disappearing into the distance running along the down line towards Kingscote. I summoned the Station Master, who in turn called the Station Foreman, they both removed their uniform jackets and ties and started off in hot pursuit. The Station Master was a Sussex League football referee but the Foreman was not so athletic. About a mile down line the now exhausted animal came to a stand on the viaduct and they managed to secure it and return to the station. An up train was due which added to the problem. Bearing in mind the state of the dog, which we established had been to stud, it was decided to place it in the cycle store to cool down before we made a call to the Dewar Estate. The Station Master and Foreman went on to the down platform and I was about to enter the Ticket Office when through the main door came the Divisional Superintendent and his Assistant. This was the 1950s and we were all reprimanded on the spot, the sweating Station Master and Foreman were improperly dressed. No mention was made of the dog, but the moral is, never loosen the collar of a greyhound

"A Pigeon problem."

Pigeons in baskets were regularly sent from one station to another for local release, the time this occurred being recorded on the label. This particular morning sometime between 7.30 am and 8.00 am, the local pigeon fancier joined the queue of early morning passengers insisting that his pigeons be forwarded by the next available service. Inconvenient as it was, I opened the parcels office door, quickly stamped up the basket and summoned Bill the Railman. Bill quickly responded and took the basket whilst I continued to deal with the queue of passengers. Our pigeon fancier lived no more than 200 yards away from the station and so after a few minutes later with all trains departed, it was a surprise to find said bird fancier again at the window. This time in quite a rage as his birds had arrived home before him. Bill was immediately summonsed and asked what he had done with the pigeons for dispatch? He replied he had indeed dispatched them and put an empty basket to return back on the train. Poor Bill, he had mixed up an arriving empty basket with the full one just received. We tried again the next the next day, but our pigeon fancier friend failed to see the funny side of the situation.

1. Sir Archibald was a New Zealand man who achieved international fame during WW2 for his pioneering work with plastic surgery on RAF air crew.

Absolutely nothing to do with East Grinstead (Southampton Central actually), but we could not resist using the space here for this view of No. 7899 'The George and Dragon', undated, but believed to be early 1951.

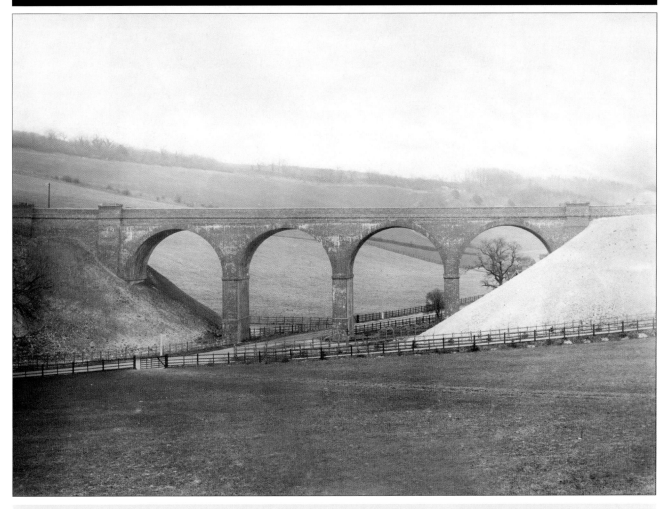

Marden Park viaduct, a little to the north of the station of the same name, which was renamed Woldingham in 1894.

This month, we feature a further selection of the photographs of the Croydon, Oxted & East Grinstead Railway taken in 1884 – the first selection was in *The Southern Way* No. 7.

These photographs were taken immediately after completion of the Croydon, Oxted & East Grinstead Railway in 1884, probably for the contractor, Joseph Firbank, and are reproduced from original contact prints made from the glass plates. A few have been copied over the years but this is the first time that most of them have been reproduced. They are of great value in showing a range of bridges and other structures when new before they were partly obscured by vegetation. There are also views of Upper Warlingham and Oxted stations, taken as part of the same series, copies of which are in the Lens of Sutton Collection, but these were not among the original prints seen here. Similar sets of views were made of the Chichester-Midhurst line and that between Oxted and Ashurst.

The Selsdon-East Grinstead line involved some heavy works, cutting as it did through the North Downs and the High Weald near East Grinstead. The section seen in the initial set of views made use of the abandoned Surrey & Sussex Junction line of the 1860s but there is nothing visible in them to indicate that the works were not completely new. The engineering works on the line as a whole included three substantial viaducts of wrought iron girders at Riddlesdown, Oxted and Cook's Pond, together with a great many lesser brick and iron bridges.

Notes by John Minnis

St Margaret's Junction, just to the north of East Grinstead station with, on the left, the line down to the Low Level station and, on the right, the line that rose steeply to the High Level station and the Three-Bridges-Tunbridge Wells line. The Saxby & Farmer signal box of the familiar pattern was opened in October 1885 and closed on 2 January 1967. Durkins Road overbridge is in the foreground, the road running past St Margaret's convent which gave the junction its name.

Looking north east towards St Margaret's Junction (the box is just visible), on the spur line linking East Grinstead High Level station with the Oxted line. On the left, the massive retaining wall (which supports the garden of Lingfield Lodge, occupied in 1884 by Dr John Whyte) abuts the bridge carrying the main London road with a pedestrian footbridge beyond it.

Looking south, this view of a bridge just to the north of Dormans station provides a rare view of the signal box, abolished on 18 December 1933.

An underbridge between Lingfield and Dormans.

Some of these photographs are fine compositions in their own right, witness this portrait of a bridge crossing road and stream near Lingfield. The little girl poses with her milk pails while, in the distance, labourers with a cow look on.

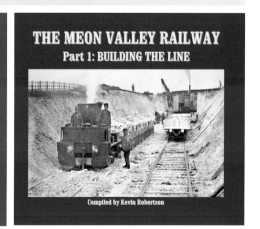

Looking south down towards Lingfield, showing, in the foreground the bridge carrying the SER Tonbridge-Redhill line and a road bridge beyond

Top - A bridge carrying the line over a stream just to the south of Crowhurst Junction.
Bottom - Looking along the line near Crowhurst Junction. This photograph illustrates perfectly the ballasting practice of the day which was to cover all but the rails in ballast. This contrasts with many views of the main line which show the sleepers exposed at the ends and gaps left every seven or eight sleepers.

Cooks Pond viaduct stood about a mile south of Dormans station and was perhaps the most impressive of the three wrought iron viaducts on the line.

BOURNEMOUTH CENTRAL 1955
A sad case of Déjà vu.

The collision which occurred at Bournemouth Central on 22 January 1955, bears a striking similarity to the events outside Victoria on 9 December 1949 - *see 'SW' No. 3 and follow up in No. 5.* In both cases a light engine was in collision with a passenger train, the main difference at Bournemouth being the movements, instead of being in the same direction they were instead opposing and it was only by good fortune that a full head on smash was avoided. Even so, the damage caused by what was a significant side swipe, was sufficient to condemn one of the engines to scrap.

As with the earlier incident, the circumstances as easily told. Around 7.45 pm on a dark January Saturday, 'H15' No.

30485 was entering the station at the head of the six coach 6.30 pm Weymouth to Waterloo passenger service. The train was running on the Up local line under clear signals allowing it to enter the platform. As it reached a point commensurate with the facing turnout leading to the Up through line, it was struck at an acute angle by a light engine, 'King Arthur' No. 30783 'Sir Gillemere'. The light engine previously having been standing on the Up through line. For reasons the driver of No. 30783 was later unable to explain, he misread the clear indication on the gantry above him, and applicable to another movement, as his own, setting off towards what was the inevitable collision course.

The two engines, both left hand drive, met offside cylin-

The morning after the night before. The fatally wounded 'H15' No. 30485 lies on its side in soft ground with the front at an angle so as to obstruct access to and from Bournemouth depot. On the right is the other engine involved, 'King Arthur' No. 30783 'Sir Gillemere', from this angle seemingly just minus the left hand smoke deflector: the latter item had been removed to facilitate lifting. It has been pulled clear and now waits at the west end of the up platform. It will later be stabled in the depot for initial assessment The Eastleigh crane is to the left, whilst behind No. 30495 the Bournemouth crane has been shunted as close as possible from within the depot. Those on the ground at the front of the engine are seemingly discussing the options available. Although not visible from the photographs, one of the first steps would have been to separate the engine and tender by cutting through the draw gear. C P Boocock

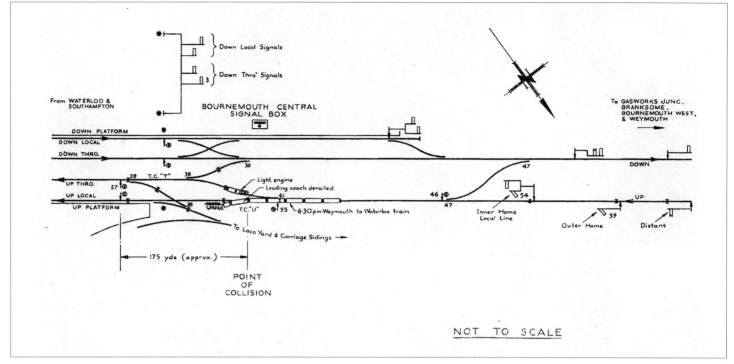

Opposite page, top - *From the other side, the damage to No. 30783 is seen to be somewhat more serious. (Apart from a new right hand cylinder subsequent repairs included the welding of a full new front end.)*   Russell Burridge
Opposite page, bottom - *Inspection of the scene and permanent way. From the debris the forces involved can only be imagined at: the torn cylinder upside down in the 'six-foot' and misshapen connecting rod. In the background is an unidentified 'B4' with the riding vehicles from one of the cranes.*   Russell Burridge

der to cylinder with considerable force. Indeed, the impact caused both to derail, more so the 'H15', which together with its tender, fell over on to its left side at an angle of 45°. The right hand cylinder of No. 30783 was completely torn off as a consequence. The front bogie of the first coach of the passenger train was also derailed and there was consequential damage, mainly to the draw gear, to four of the other five coaches. There was slight injury to one passenger and four members of the "engine and train crew", one, the fireman of the Weymouth train, was detained in hospital.

To make matters worse, No. 30485 had come to rest completely blocking the entrance / exit from the depot at Bournemouth where 15 steam engines were effectively marooned. Within the depot the point of the derailment, had according the inspectors report, also rendered the normal coal and watering facilities unusable. In addition, both Up lines into the station were now blocked for any traffic approaching from the direction of Branksome and Bournemouth West, whilst in addition traffic would quickly pile up from the east coming from Brockenhurst. This was all cleared as quickly as possible and single line working introduced over the two miles between Bournemouth Central and Gas Works Junction, the nearest signal box to the west of the station, at 10.05 pm.

Mr Pringle, the Bournemouth Shedmaster, requested two breakdown cranes, those normally based at Eastleigh and Salisbury. Fortuitously, the Eastleigh crane was already on the way even before the accident happened. It had been scheduled to leave Eastleigh at 6.00 pm together with a brake van and proceed to Dorchester Exchange Sidings where it was to work "As ordered by the D.O.S., Bristol" on what was in effect a regular se-

ries of weekend bridge replacements. At the time of the actual accident, 7.45 pm, the special traffic notice applicable to this original movement has the crane as between Christchurch and Bournemouth, so assuming it was running to schedule, it would literally have been approaching or even in the station when the accident occurred. But the Eastleigh crane on its own needed the assistance of its associated full crew complement and equipment contained in the running vans. These had not been taken on the initial planned trip to Dorchester, so whilst they were summoned, the Eastleigh crane was sent to turn on the Branksome triangle, the full ensemble reported as ready for work by 11.18 pm.

According to the official report, the Salisbury steam crane was initially sent to Dorchester to cover the CCE Dept work, although this is contradicted by Bill Bishop in his reminiscences' book 'OFF THE RAILS'[1]. In this he recounts that the Salisbury crane was in fact held at Poole in case it was needed and it was from here that it was eventually summoned back to Bournemouth. Whatever, we know it finally arrived at Bournemouth at 1.00pm on Sunday.

As a preliminary task to the restoration, the rear five coaches of the passenger train were first drawn clear, although no comment about how this might have been achieved with the damaged draw-gear is given - possibly temporary screw couplings were used. The fires on both the locomotives would also have been drawn, Bournemouth men no doubt detailed for this task. No attempt at re-railing could commence until 2.45 am on the Sunday morning, at which point all scheduled east - west traffic had been dealt with. (Not mentioned is the possibility that the 'old road' via Ringwood may well have been used as a diversion-

Signal No. 3

Route taken by No. 30783

A panoramic view from the vantage point of Bournemouth central signal box. The gantry with No. 3 signal, the one misread by Driver Thorne, is indicated. The engine in the distance is standing at the same point as the light engine for which No. 3 signal was intended. No. 30783 was on the line immediately left and set off on its collision course on to the rails where the man is to the right of the Eastleigh crane - also indicated. The view was taken after the abortive first lift and at which point the engine was at least upright again but before the arrival of the Salisbury crane as seen opposite.
C P Boocock

ary route.) Even so, due to unspecified 'unforeseen difficulties', the one derailed coach was not put back on to the rails until 5.50 a.m. and then with the combined assistance of the breakdown crews from both depots.

The Eastleigh crane on its own then dealt with re-railing the light engine, the 'King Arthur', but restoring the 'H15' required two cranes and for this purpose the Bournemouth crane was shunted as close as possible from the depot side and chains secured for a side lift. The Eastleigh crane took position at the rear. In this way the engine was moved to a more upright position, at which point the chains from the Bournemouth crane failed. According to Bill Bishop, this was because they were attempting to lift more weight than was realised. Fortunately the Eastleigh crane was able to retain the engine in its upright position.

In charge of the recovery at this stage was Mr. Thompson, the recently promoted District Superintendent. He immediately summoned the Salisbury crane and with two large cranes now in action the engine was successfully re-railed by 3.25 pm. After this matters moved fast, double line working was re-established at 6.32 pm, by which time temporary repairs had also been made to the track. Even so trains were hand-signalled

through the damaged area until 4.30 pm on Monday when full normal working was resumed. The clean-up having taken just over 44 hours to achieve.

Naturally there was an enquiry, most of the facts quoted above coming from the Ministry of Transport report of 3 March 1955. Col. D. McMullen was in charge and uncovered a basic catalogue of human error, the start of which may even laid at the door of the Bournemouth Central signalman, H. Dorey, although it must be explained, no formal blame was ever attached to this man.

Dorey had accepted the light engine but admitted he was unaware as to its next duty. We are not told where it had originated from, but as it passed his signal box he realised it was due to take a subsequent train from Bournemouth Central the short distance to Bournemouth West. Consequently, having first accepted the engine and signalled it into the main Up platform: shortly to be needed for the train from Weymouth, he cleared the route for it to retrace its steps the short distance into the carriage sidings and then reverse direction yet again to a stand off position at the west end of the Up through line. (The fact he had first placed the engine in the up platform is indicative of a belief it may have been destined for the shed.) Dorey's actions were all

The Eastleigh (left) and Salisbury (right) steam cranes in action with No. 30485. The time would have been sometime after 2.25 pm on Monday 24 January, as reports indicate the two big cranes took less than one hour to rerail the engine. Passing by cautiously 'wrong-line' on the down through line but in the up direction and about to enter the down platform, is a 76xxx on a working from Weymouth.

C P Boocock

perfectly legitimate, even if more than half a century later it seems a somewhat convoluted behaviour from an experienced signalman who might be expected to know the next movement he could expect.

Dorey had in effect three simultaneous workings to consider. Firstly the now stationary light engine, secondly the approaching passenger train from Weymouth: which he had accepted perfectly legitimately and was scheduled to arrive under clear signals, and also at the west end of the station, a departing light engine for Branksome. This departing engine had come off a terminated passenger service which had left its now empty stock in the down through line. (We are not given any further details of this train.) This engine left Bournemouth under a clear signal, a signal located on the gantry above where Driver Thorne was waiting on the 'King Arthur' and it was the clearing of this signal, No. 3 on the diagram, that was misinterpreted by Thorne as applicable to him. On Thorne setting off in this way the consequences were inevitable, his true signal, a ground signal on the right hand side of the engine and which when cleared would have permitted legitimate access from the up through to the down through line, was still displaying the 'stop' indication.

The last line of defence was the fireman on the 'King Arthur', a 16 year old Passed Cleaner, M. R. Standhaft. Both

crew totally corroborated each others account, including that upon arriving on the Up through line, Standhaft had advised his driver the ground signal was at danger, which Thorne checked for himself. They also both admitted No. 3 was later cleared to the 'off' position. The fact the fireman had advised his driver the ground signal was originally 'on' clearly shows both crew knew this signal was applicable to them, yet, when the driver moved the engine forward, it appears the fireman did not re-check its indication, had he done so he might have been able to warn the driver. This point was not lost on Col. McMullen.

Speed was not an issue, although the driver of the 'H15' thought he was probably travelling at only a little less than 25 mph at the time of the accident. The geography of the scene, a slight left hand curve approaching the station from the west, also meant that the driver of the 'H15' (we are not given his name), would have had little advance warning of the obstruction until almost the last moment. Even then it would also only have been by seeing the headlights of the 'King Arthur'. There was nothing unusual in this and no extraneous circumstances or weather conditions to consider.

For his part Driver Thorne could not explain his actions. Here was a man with a previous excellent record, an experienced driver, who could only state that as his initial arrival at Bourne-

Opposite, top left - The abortive first lift, with the Bournemouth carne attempting recovery from a less than ideal angle. This was as close as it could manoeuvre at this time.

C P Boocock

Opposite page, top right - A view along the right hand side of No. 30783

C P Boocock

Opposite page, bottom - Three cranes visible, although only two will play a part in the actual lift. It must be realised that whilst the point of collision is indicated on the plan, No. 30485 did not come to a dead stop as a result but continued on for perhaps a further 100 feet or so, in the process turning over to the left. It was at the point it came to rest that the depot exit was fouled. Re-railing of No. 30783 had been accomplished during the early morning, sometime after 5.50 am, and probably the reason why there are no photographs of this engine in its derailed position. In the background, the engine at the extreme left, has all the appearance of a 'Z' class 0-8-0T!

C P Boocock

This page, top - The runner of DS35, the Eastleigh crane is just visible in this view of the scene. The Bournemouth crane is in position for its abortive lift and DS35 will shortly draw forward. Several Trilby hats and railway issue coats are visible in this and other illustrations.

C P Boocock

This page, middle - Watched by a crowd from the south end of the down platform, No. 30485 regains the rails. Bill Bishop recalled that with the job complete, Mr Thompson adopted his former LMR practice of treating all those involved to lunch. This was taken in the South Western Hotel.

Russell Burridge

This page, bottom - A final view of the off-side cylinder from No. 30783. This has not only come to rest upside down but has also 'rolled' through 180°.

Russell Burridge

1. Kingfisher Railway Productions, 1984. 0946184062. reprinted Bracken Books 1988. 1851702083.

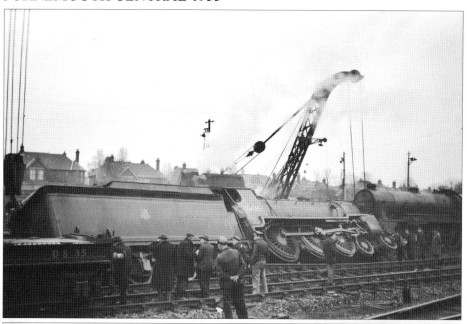

A serene summer day at Bournemouth Central a few years beforehand. 15 August 1959 sees 'M7' tank. No 318 waiting in the carriage sidings with a pull-push working.

mouth and consequent two shunt movements to reach his stabling point had been completed quickly, he may well have assumed he was to depart again equally quickly. In reality we may conclude the reason for this haste was for Dorey to clear the route as quickly as possible - pending the arrival of the passenger working. We are not told at what time Thorne would have been due to next depart from Bournemouth, nor what, if any, communication - and if yes how this was achieved, had taken place between Thorne and Dorey.

At the time the engine commenced to move, Fireman Standhaft was apparently re-lighting the gauge lamp, with this accomplished he looked forward to see the oncoming train. His shout of warning was enough to alert his driver, possibly even to ensure the engine was stationary at the time of impart, although by creating a terrible obstruction. We may conclude then Standhaft did not check the indication given by the ground signal as the engine commenced to move forward.

Col. McMullen had no option but to lay the blame at Driver Thorne, although with the rider, "The driver was certainly not helped by his fireman". Standhaft, although young, had already amassed some 155 firing turns and in the report it was stated , "...he knew Bournemouth station well." However a little later that same comment is almost contradicted as, "Standhaft said that he did not know all the Bournemouth Central signals, but that he did know the difference between running and shunting signals". (Disc No. 27 had two separate functions dependent upon how the actual route was set: 'Up Through to Loco yard and Up Through to Down Through Starting.') It was a case of the driver having to shoulder the blame as indeed in percentage terms he cannot avoid the major share of culpability, although in so doing the actions of the others involved become hidden rather than placed alongside, albeit at a justifiably lower level.

So far as the locomotives were concerned, both were quickly hauled to Eastleigh for assessment. No. 30783 'Sir Gillemere', at the time a Bournemouth allocated machine, was repaired and lasted until March 1961. Not so for 'H15' No. 30485 of Nine Elms, already considered to be due for early withdrawal, Thus No. 30485 languished, notionally at least, 'on the books' until April, when it was formally condemned, the first of the class to be withdrawn. We can be certain it would never have worked again after the 22 January.

Reference the item opposite - "... and speaking of the 'King Arthur' class, we were delighted to receive this view as well. A somewhat rare image, not of Driver Fred (well not that we know of), but instead the footplate of an oil-burning 'King Arthur', the control for the latter fuel in the left hand of the Fireman."

David Ballard collection.

'DRIVER FRED'

This is the tale of Driver Fred
Inmate of rural engine shed
Who daily drove an express train
To Waterloo and home again
Midst shouts from passengers irate
Who said the train was always late
And with an engine called "King Arthur"
Ought to go a darned sight faster.

At last the foreman sent for Fred
And seated in his office said
"Why not run your train to time,
Not crawl along and block the line?"
The travelling public do not pay
To die of old age on the way"

Said Fred "How can I do my stuff?
The engine aint half big enough
The train is long and getting longer;
My poor old engine gets no stronger.
Give us a streamlined engine or
We won't come in to work no more".

This fairly gave the staff the jitters
The foreman sent for various fitters
Said "This is a right to do,
There'll be no train to Waterloo
Lest for our Fred we manage to find
An engine what he calls Streamlined

Up spoke a lad in greasy jacket
"Why not give him Channel Packet?"
But when they went to look they found
This loco was the wrong way round
So 'stead of off to Town with Fred
It went to Exeter instead

Then spoke another lad 'mid laughter
"Why not camouflage his old King Arthur?"

"Ah" said foreman "that might do it
Get out your tools and all go to it.
That night when Fred were safe at home
They cut off chimney; cut off dome

And with a hammer and a Chisel
Even sliced off half the whistle.
Then did it up with lumps of boarding
Filched from an adjacent hoarding
And though in size it showed some lack, it
Did look like the Channel Packet.

Came the dawn and also Fred
Who (when he got inside the shed)
Found all the staff a flocking round
Eager to show him what they'd found.
He much to everyone's surprise
His engine failed to recognise

He murmured with uplifted stare
"The answer to a driver's prayer"
Said to his mate with nasty snigger
"See what we'll with summat bigger"
He drove to Town and home again,
There never was a faster train.

The station staff was most excited
The passengers highly delighted
He who they used to curse, poor man
Was told he ought to be Foreman
But Fred weren't having none of that
He hadn't got a bowler hat.

So daily drives to Town and Home
Without a chimney or a dome
So that's; the end of that
Althoo it only goes to show
Or do it???

We were alerted to the above by reader Derek Brooker, which he recalls copying from the *SOUTHERN RAILWAY MAGAZINE* circa 1942. (Alastair Wilson comments it could be a pastiche of one of the late Cyril Fletcher's "Odd Odes" - very popular at the time.)
It might be said to have been intended as a morale booster from the period, whilst displaying a marked similarity in style to some modern day composers of prose. In factual terms it may be slightly inaccurate - it was of course a 'Schools' not an 'Arthur;' that was streamlined and even then only as a test and not for revenue earning service. But does that matter, we think not. As a piece of fun it is quite delightful.

Flooding at Reculver, east of Herne Bay, the sea wall breached and track displaced, as recorded on 2 February 1953.

FLOODING IN NORTH KENT 1953

David Monk-Steel

On the night of Saturday 31 January through to Sunday 1 February 1953 a deep depression moved east-south-east from south of Iceland, and then turned rapidly south into the North Sea. At the same time pressure rose west of Ireland. The outcome was a steep pressure gradient across the British Isles. This pressure difference created gales and heavy driving rain across southern and eastern England. High winds were uprooting trees and damaging buildings along the eastern side of Britain. The low pressure allowed the sea level in the North Sea to rise above normal, and this coupled with an exceptionally high tide, two days after the Spring tide, caused the sea level to overtop the sea defences from the Humber to North Foreland, including the Wash and the Thames Estuary. The coastal districts of Lincolnshire and East Anglia suffered initially: worst hit were Sutton, Mablethorpe, Kings Lynn, Hunstanton, Cromer, Great Yarmouth, Felixstowe, Harwich, and Clacton. Town centres were flooded, resulting in 25,000 houses under water and regrettably 307 persons lost their lives. Many railway lines were severely affected, and on the evening of the 31 January near Hunstanton a local train to Kings Lynn was in collision with a substantial part of a bungalow that had floated away on the flood water. As the tidal surge entered the Thames Estuary it continued to cause flooding, and damage on both sides of the river occurred all the way to the outskirts of London. Canvey Island in Essex was devastated, 58 persons lost their lives.

Nine places on the Southern Region Eastern Section suffered flood damage. At Birchington the earth and clay sea wall which was between ¼ and ½ mile from the railway was breached in two places each approximately 1,000 yards long and the concrete wall overtopped. The low lying marsh land between the sea wall and railway filled with water. This then poured through the culverts and bridges under the railway and continued on to flood to the Thanet Way coast trunk road. Between Reculver (66½ milepost) and Birchington (69 miles 25 chains) the flood water seriously distorted the track and washed away the ballast, and in places the embankment as well. Platelayers' huts were destroyed and two bridges were damaged. The damage to the railway was extensive and restoration would take three months.

At Graveney, east of Faversham, the earth and clay sea wall which was between 100 yards and 1½ miles from the railway was breached in several places and the concrete wall overtopped. Between the 55½ milepost and 56¾ milepost there was heavy damage to permanent way including some ballast and embankments washed out. The fences suffered damage, and here too some platelayers' huts were destroyed. The line was blocked for 22 days, repairs finally being completed on Thursday 19 February. Engineering trains then ran to prepare the crossovers for temporary operations of both the chalk trains and the shuttle services. On Monday 23 February single-line working was instituted and the line opened for engineering trains to pass over the repaired section at 10 mph to take chalk to site. Further repairs

were effected to restore double line during the next seven days and a shuttle service of passenger trains started on Monday 2 March. The 10 mph restriction remained in force until the middle of April.

The timber quay wall of Whitstable Harbour was damaged. Some scour and damage to the concrete apron occurred. It did not affect the train services which had ceased in the previous year.

At Queenborough several short breaches of the earth and clay sea wall took place, allowing flood water to damage the Sheerness branch in three places. There was heavy damage to the permanent way and fencing between the 46¼ milepost & 47½ milepost, between 47¾ milepost & 48½ milepost and also between 49½ milepost & 50¾ milepost. Embankments were scoured and platelayers' huts were damaged or destroyed. The flooding had also severed the roads on to the island. Much of Sheerness was under water. One grisly aspect of the flood was the toll of livestock. On Monday 9 February and Tuesday 10 February steam crane No. 341S and two open wagons were booked to work in daylight hours between Kemsley and Swale loading dead animals. No service at all operated until Saturday 14 February when a 'bus service calling at all stations was started. The line between Sittingbourne and Queenborough was repaired sufficiently to permit trains to operate at 10 mph by Monday 23 February with a 'bus connection into Sheerness, and trains ran through to Sheerness at 10 mph by Monday 2 March. The speed restriction was lifted in mid-April.

The earth and clay embankment sea defences of the Isle of Grain were breached in 49 places. At Grain Halt the track of the Port Victoria branch was distorted for one mile, and banks and ballast washed out to a depth of up to 4 feet. 1½ miles of fence was destroyed and a further 1½ miles damaged. Platelayers' huts were damaged or destroyed. The Allhallows-on-Sea branch was inundated. Point and crossing work was distorted and ¾ mile of track undermined. ½ mile of fencing was destroyed and a further ½ mile was damaged. The line to the Isle of Grain oil refinery was opened to permit a light diesel engine to operate by Tuesday 17th February. The whole branch including the line to Allhallows-on-Sea was re-opened at 20 mph from Monday 2 March. Normal operations resumed on Tuesday 31 March.

Water penetrated Strood Tunnel when the River Medway overtopped the quay walls of Strood Dock. Between 29½ milepost and 30 miles 17 chains the formation in the tunnel under the track was softened and declared unsafe. The line was re-opened the following day with a 5 mph temporary speed restriction. The speed restriction was relaxed to 30 mph on 9 February. Normal working resumed over the up line on Thursday 12 February and over the down line on Monday 16 February.

Further up the River Thames at Belvedere the earth river defence embankments were breached in several places between Erith and Woolwich. Between the 12½ milepost and 13½ mile-

Top - Reculver again and a displaced Platelayer's hut.
Bottom - 'Kent Floods Poster No. 1', recorded at Horsham, 3 April 1953. *The Lens of Sutton Collection.*

post the flood waters softened the formation, and washed ballast out 6 inches beneath the sleepers. Trains ran from London to Abbey Wood and between Erith and Dartford (or beyond) with some diverted via the Dartford Loop or Bexleyheath lines. Passengers to Belvedere were directed to use London Transport 'bus and trolley-bus services which accepted train tickets. The flood water remained for 9 days. Trains resumed on Tuesday 10 but a 5 mph temporary speed restriction was imposed. Only the Charing Cross to Gillingham services reverted to this route at first and the local services remained curtailed. On Saturday 14 February the

line speed was raised to 20 mph and a full train service was reinstated. Normal working resumed on Friday 20 February.

Deptford Wharf sustained a 15 foot breach of the concrete wall. The flood water caused minor damage and silted up the track. The flood did however back up the River Ravensbourne. Southern Region Eastern Section electric suburban services drew power supplies from the London Electricity Supply Co's generating station at Deptford. This suffered flood damage and train services were reduced to conserve power. The 'Fog' working service was implemented, and despite it being early February 2-BIL, 2-NOL, 2-HAL and 4-SUB units ran without heat! Notices warning passengers were displayed prominently.

The effects were also felt the other side of the Dover Strait, in Sussex. Newhaven Harbour quay wall was overtopped but fortunately no damage occurred. One fact that could give some comfort was that because the high tide reached the Kent coast after midnight on Saturday night there were no trains on the affected sections at the time and no railway staff in Kent suffered injury whilst on duty.

Away from the railway, Margate suffered considerable damage both from the high seas and the gales, a Royal Navy frigate in Sheerness dockyard capsized and a submarine was torn from its moorings. Across the North Sea Holland and Belgium also suffered severe flooding and loss of life.

The Kent Rivers Board and Port of London Authority were successful in repairing most of the damage to the sea defences as the flood tide subsided, although some flooding did return on successive tides for a few days. However at Belvedere the flooding took nine days to recede and between Reculver and Birchington the damage was so severe that a major civil engineering project would be needed to restore the defences and repair the damage.

The Reculver to Birchington breach took a long time and a great deal of effort to restore. The sea wall was breached in several places and over 5000 acres of land was under water on either side of the railway. Damage to the railway embankment stretched for 1¾ miles over the marshes, with track either washed away or seriously distorted.

The original sea wall was temporarily repaired but it was not considered that this would guarantee permanent protection, and so the Kent Rivers Board decided to construct a new sea wall consisting of a 14 foot high chalk embankment. It was to be just north of the railway and parallel with it across Reculver marshes to supplement the existing sea wall. To do this a large quantity of chalk would be necessary and because road access to the site was severely limited, the bulk of the chalk would have to be brought in by rail. Once this second wall was completed and the railway and trunk road adequately defended, the original sea defences could be strengthened to safeguard the agricultural land in between. This task was estimated to last three years.

Suitable chalk quarries were identified at Manston near Ramsgate, and Knockholt south of Orpington. Both were serviceable by rail. The Railway Executive co-ordinated the quarrying and transportation which required some land purchase, the construction of an access line 1000 yards long at Ramsgate and extra sidings at both locations. Mechanical excavators were to be used to quarry the chalk and load railway wagons.

The former down line, using the displaced permanent way material was restored as a single service line between Reculver and Birchington, to facilitate the delivery of chalk. Scaffold towers were erected to support floodlighting driven by portable generators at 75 yard intervals along the worksite. New crossovers were provided at each end to facilitate the working.

At Reculver the double line became single at a set of hand points operated by the guard. The engineers had occupation from Reculver's down home signal and all movements were controlled by hand signals. Crossover connection at Reculver between the up and down lines permitted engines to run round the train. For some weeks at Herne Bay the train was divided into two portions on arrival and each taken to site separately, and after discharge the two portions were returned to Herne Bay and reformed. Trains were hauled to site and after unloading were propelled to Reculver where the run round could be carried out. A similar arrangement was adopted at Birchington for trains wishing to enter the site at that end. The points for the run round at Birchington were operated by the guard.

On Sunday 29 March a trial was carried out using a locomotive at both ends of trains going on to site from Reculver, but no advantages in working were obtained and the original working was retained.

Two mechanical 'truck dischargers', which were diesel excavators modified to drag chalk from inside the drop side wagons, was delivered to site on a 'Crocodile' bogie well wagon on Sunday 22 February.

In the first week, 23 February to 28 February, 100 trains delivered 15,000 tons of chalk. Over the whole 44 days from 23 February nearly 200,000 tons of chalk were delivered in 750 trains, usually formed of up to 40 drop sided wagons and two brake-vans.

From 24 February two trains of nine ex-GWR side tipping 'Mermaid' wagons with a brake-van at either end moved chalk from Ramsgate to Birchington. 35 pathways a day for these trains were allocated between Ramsgate and Birchington, each trip taking approximately half an hour. These wagons transferred from the WR on Friday 20 February via Woking and Tonbridge. They were booked to be conveyed on 11:48 am Woking to Tonbridge, 7:57 pm Tonbridge to Ashford, and 3:45 am (Sat) Ashford to Margate. Until the crossovers were installed a turn-over locomotive was provided. Later a train of 25 drop-sided wagons was introduced to increase capacity. The last train of chalk from Ramsgate ran on Friday 17 April at 4:55 am.

Chalk trains ran day and night, seven day a week. As an example the following extracted from the Special Traffic Notice for 23 February shows trains departed Knockholt for Reculver at the following times. Loads were 20 'ADS' wagons to Chislehurst and 40 'ADS' wagons to Faversham, although if an 'N' class locomotive was used the load to Faversham might be increased to 60 wagons. Single line working applied from Graveney to Reculver. At Herne Bay trains were divided into two portions before being propelled to site. All movements on site were controlled by hand signal, and the guard was to travel in the leading brake-van during the propelling movement. After discharge the portions were hauled to Herne Bay to be reformed for the return trip. From observation, the term 'ADS' indicated a three plank height open wagon, with full length drop doors, of the kind coded 'Medium' or 'Medfit' or departmental equivalent.

WEEKDAYS FROM 24 FEBRUARY							
Depart Knockholt	Days run	Chislehurst Goods Arr.	Chislehurst Goods dep.	Faversham Arr.	Faversham Dep.	Reculver Arr.	Return empty at.
11:20pm		11:40 pm					
2 am	MX	2:20 am	4:10 am	6:46 am	7:15 am	8 am	10:20 am
5 am	MX	5:20 am					
7:25 am	MX	7:45 am	10:7 am	12:38 pm SX 1:20 pm SO	1:30 pm	2:50 pm	5:15 pm
11:48 am	MX	12:8 pm					
2:20 pm	MX	2:40 pm	3 pm	5:33 pm SX 5:24 pm SO	6:40 pm	8 pm	10:20 pm
7 pm		7:20 pm					
9:18 pm		9:38 pm	10 pm	12:20 am	5:20 am	6:36 am	8 am

This page - *The chalk quarry at Knockholt, south of Orpington. This was one of two new sites identified as a source of material: the other was at Manston near Ramsgate.*

Opposite - *Unloading at Birchington.*

Top - No. 30770 'Sir Prianius' loading chalk at Manston, February / March 1953.   Milepost 92½/ A W V Mace Collection.
Bottom - Ballast at Clapham Junction. ***Opposite page*** *- Poster No. 2, Birchington , 19 April 1953.*   The Lens of Sutton Collection.

There were also four trains to Faversham on Sundays. Trains reformed at Chislehurst Goods, and were then hauled to Reculver via Sole Street and Faversham, returning the same way. Some trains were sent by alternative routes to avoid conflicts with business trains, or were staged at Faversham or Hoo Junction to balance out resources.

There was a 'Q' path from Knockholt at 10:22 am introduced on 2 March, and as soon as the double line was restored the timings of the chalk trains were improved to allow six departures from Chislehurst Goods at 1:10 am, 4:10 am, 10:7 am, 3 pm, 9:2 pm and 11:2 pm. The 2:20 pm chalk train from Knockholt was retimed to 2:58 pm, and the 9:18 pm was replaced by a departures at 8:48 pm from that date. With minor changes this remained broadly the pattern of service until the repairs were completed.

A 350hp diesel shunting locomotive was sent by Hither Green to shunt the sidings at Knockholt. Motive power for the chalk trains was a mixture mainly of 'N15' 4-6-0 and 'N' 2-6-0, and occasionally 'C' 0-6-0, and 'W' 2-6-4T were seen particularly between Knockholt and Chislehurst Goods, but subsequently four 'Q1' 0-6-0s, Nos. 33002, 33004, 33005 & 33016 were loaned to Faversham and three more, 33007, 33009, and 33011 were loaned to Hither Green for this traffic. Hither Green already had Nos. 33014, 33015, and 33037.

On 25 April it was considered that the sea wall was completed sufficiently to allow the permanent way to be reinstated. Chalk trains from Knockholt had ceased to run from Wednesday 8 April although filling, grading and consolidating work continued on site for the next few weeks, and the formation was handed to the permanent way department. From then 12,000 cu yards of ballast from Meldon and four miles of new track from Ashford were brought to site on 60 engineer's 'ballast' trains. A train was despatched from Ashford on Wednesday 22 April to recover the generators used on the lighting towers. The repairs were finally complete on 20 May.

Whilst all this work was proceeding it was necessary to provide alternative services. Immediately after the disaster on Sunday a replacement motor 'bus service was provided serving Birchington, Herne Bay, Whitstable and Faversham. The road journey from Birchington to Faversham calling at all stations took one hour (25 minutes longer than normal).

On Monday 2 February a plan was formulated, although it was not fully achieved. Some trains from Ramsgate which normally ran via Faversham were diverted over the Kearsney Loop and via Canterbury East, these included the 3:20 pm 4:15 pm, 5:5 pm, 7:45 pm and 9:10 pm Ramsgate to Victoria, 3:35 pm, 7:35 pm, 8:35 pm and 9:35 pm Victoria to Ramsgate, and 4:45 pm 5:15 pm, 5:45 pm 6:15 pm Cannon Street to Ramsgate. Additional trains for Cannon Street departed Faversham. An additional train was run via Ashford to Cannon Street departing Margate at 6:55 am. A few trains were curtailed or restarted at Faversham. Delay was considerable with the 'bus at least ½ hour late by Whitstable. On Monday 2 February 'buses operated to Canterbury East from Herne Bay and Whitstable. On that day the 8:19am from Canterbury East despite strengthening left passengers behind. Goods services were severely disrupted.

A further revision was instituted on Tuesday 3 reducing the number of diverted trains, terminating or starting them at Fav-

ersham and replacing them with a further number of 'buses between there and Birchington. A shuttle service of trains ran at approximately hourly intervals between Birchington and Ramsgate. Fine tuning of the timetable continued throughout that week and into the following two.

The importance of parcels, mails and sundries traffic was not overlooked. Road services to North Kent and the Isle of Sheppey met the 3 am Holborn Viaduct to Ramsgate which terminated at Faversham, and the 3:50 am Victoria to Ramsgate which had been diverted.

The Canterbury and Whitstable branch, closed on 1 December 1952, was re-opened temporarily on 5 February to take coal and other goods to Whitstable. R1 0-6-0T locomotives returned to North Kent once again, with Nos. 31339, 31010 and 31047 appearing on the daily goods trip. Some demolition had already occurred but nothing that would seriously hinder this operation.

A World War One spur between the former London Chatham and Dover route between Faversham and Dover Priory and the South Eastern route from Ashford and Minster was hastily re-instated to allow the passage of Margate and Ramsgate business trains via Chatham. It had been provided initially in 1918, opening on 5 May, to facilitate military stores trains to and

Work in progress at Reculvers with the new chalk bank facing Margate. The modern earth mover makes for an interesting comparison with the SECR trolley.
The Lens of Sutton Collection.

'W' No. 31913 on the 2.20 pm Chislehurst - Knockholt chalk empties (- having reversed at Chislehurst Goods), seen at Petts Wood junction, 28 March 1953. Apart from tank engines, a variety of locomotive classes were seen on these workings including 2-6-0 and 0-6-0 types.
The Lens of Sutton Collection.

from Richborough, and was closed on 21 November 1924, and remained in position until 1935. Following the outbreak of war in 1939, it was reinstated on 2 March 1941 to permit the large rail guns that had been stationed in East Kent to reach the coast by alternative routes. Closure for a second time occurred on 21 October 1951. The signal boxes and signals were removed but the rails were still in situ when the flooding occurred. Work started quickly and the original single line was connected on 8 February, trains of new rails departed Ashford at 7:50 am on Monday 9 February, arriving at the site at about 8:30 am: on Tuesday 10 a similar train, this time loaded with sleepers, also ran. The new up line was in position and connected on the 15. The loop was therefore recommissioned as a double line, where previously it had been single, with double junctions and full signalling at both ends. Run-off trap points were installed at the Canterbury West end of the up and down loops but the former trap points on the down loop (formerly the single line) protecting the down Dover line and the former crossovers remained clipped and padlocked out of use. Two signal boxes were constructed to operate the points and signals. Canterbury Junction 'A' was situated between Chartham Crossing and Canterbury East, and Canterbury Junction 'B' was located between Chartham and Canterbury West. The loop was fully commissioned on Sunday 22 February 1953. After the North Kent line was re-instated and normal working resumed the loop was taken out of use, and stood derelict for a number of years, finally being abolished on Sunday 12 February 1956. Freight trains were limited to 40 wagons over the new loop.

Until the Canterbury loop was commissioned trains had to travel via Deal and the Kearsney Loop where the severe gradients to Guston tunnel and Martin Mill necessitated assistance to heavy passenger expresses, and two 'D1' 4-4-0s including No. 31470 were noted performing this duty.

From Monday 23 February the North Kent train services started from Birchington and ran via Margate, calling all stations to Ramsgate and then fast to Faversham via the new loop. Because the train started its journey in Thanet the 'wrong' way the timings were significantly different, but most trains were timed to pick up the booked path from Faversham. The train was usually worked between Birchington and Ramsgate by a local Ramsgate locomotive booked to be an 'H' 0-4-4T but often a 'C' 0-6-0. The train engine was attached there for the onward journey to London.

A connecting 'bus met each of these trains starting at Herne Bay on weekdays with some services also starting back at Margate to give a connection from there to intermediate stations.

From Monday 2nd March the buses between Herne Bay and Faversham were replaced by a timetabled service of push &

pull trains. The buses were retained between Herne Bay and Margate. East Kent motor services supplied the vehicles.

At Faversham a new crossover was installed to allow the passenger shuttle to run directly from the up Ramsgate line to the down slow line. It was brought into use on Friday 28 March. It was subsequently removed on Sunday 1 August 1954.

The Motor Train operation which was instituted on 2nd March between Faversham and Herne Bay was in the hands of ex-LCDR class 'R' Push-Pull fitted 0-4-4T Nos. 31660 (Gillingham) & 31671 (Tonbridge), SECR class 'H' 0-4-4T Nos. 31161 (Ashford), 31518 (St. Leonards) & 31519 (Ramsgate) and on 15 March these were joined by LSWR class M7 0-4-4T Nos. 30052 (Fratton), 30053 (Fratton) and 30129 (Yeovil), the first time this class had penetrated so far east. All these were allocated to Faversham.

There were three locomotives required on weekdays, Faversham diagrams 265, 266 and 267 each nominally a 1PT (R1 class) P&P fitted. They worked as follows: (w/c 9 March 1953 Monday to Friday) –

DIAGRAM No. 265			DIAGRAM No. 266			DIAGRAM No. 267		
From	Depart at	Set	From	Depart at	Set	From	Depart at	Set
Faversham	4†30 am	P&P	Faversham	5†6 am	P&P	Faversham	6†5 am	2 P&P
Herne Bay	5:12 am	2 P&P	Herne Bay	7:3 am	2 P&P	Herne Bay	6:41 am	2 P&P
Faversham	7:25 am	3	Faversham	7†40 am	2 P&P	Faversham	7†10 am	2 P&P
Herne Bay	7:59 am	3	Herne Bay	8:13 am	2 P&P	Herne Bay	7:38 am	2 P&P
Faversham	9:57 am	P&P	Faversham	8†45 am	2 P&P	Faversham	8:10 am	2 P&P
Herne Bay	10†30 am	P&P	Herne Bay	9:20 am	P&P	Herne Bay	8:47 am	2 P&P
Faversham	11:4 am	P&P	Faversham	12:5 pm	P&P	Faversham	9:22 am	2 P&P
Herne Bay	11:56 am	P&P	Herne Bay	12†37 pm	P&P	Herne Bay	10:17 am	P&P
Faversham	2:15 pm	P&P	Faversham	1:10 pm	P&P	Faversham	1†50 pm	P&P
Herne Bay	4:5 pm	2 P&P	Herne Bay	1:40 pm	P&P	Herne Bay	2:29 pm	P&P
Faversham	5:2 pm	2 P&P	Faversham	8:5 pm	P&P	Faversham	4:6 pm	2 P&P
Herne Bay	5:33 pm	2 P&P	Herne Bay	8†40 pm	P&P	Herne Bay	5:1 pm	2 P&P
Faversham	6:22 pm	2 P&P	Faversham	10:7 pm	P&P	Faversham	5:52 pm	2 P&P
Herne Bay	6:54 pm	2 P&P	Herne Bay	10†40 pm	P&P	Herne Bay	6:21 pm	2 P&P
Faversham	7:26 pm	P&P				Faversham	7 pm	2 P&P
Herne Bay	8:20 pm	P&P				Herne Bay	7:30 pm	P&P
						Faversham	8:56 pm	P&P
						Herne Bay	10:8 pm	P&P
						Faversham	10:57 pm	P&P
						Herne Bay	11†30 pm	P&P

Notes : † indicates an empty train, P&P is a two coach push & pull fitted set, 2P&P is a pair of sets usually with the locomotive in between, 3 is a SECR Birdcage trio.

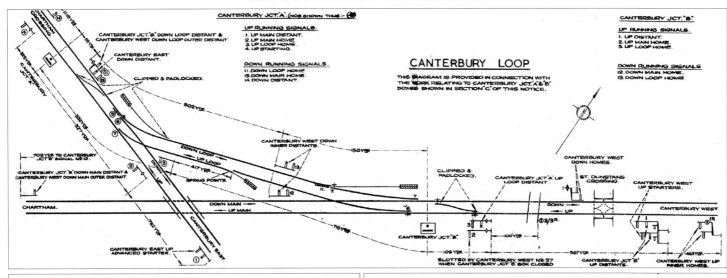

CANTERBURY JUNCTION "B" BOX

Canterbury Jc. "B" Signal Box, situated on the Up side between Canterbury West and Chartham, will again be brought into use.

The Trailing Points in the Down Main Line leading from the Down Loop Line, 6 yards Chartham side of Signal Box, together with the trap points in the Down Loop Line, 66 yards Canterbury Jc. "A" side of Signal box, at present clipped and padlocked in the normal position, will be connected up and worked from the Signal Box. The sand drag at the trap points will also be brought into use.

New Facing Points leading to the new Up Loop Line will be provided in the Up Main Line, 19 yards Chartham side of Signal Box.

The Facing Crossover Road between Down and Up Main Lines, 50 yards Canterbury West side of Signal Box, will remain clipped and padlocked in the normal position.

The undermentioned Signals will be brought into use :—

	Distance from Box
Down Loop Distant Signal (beneath Canterbury Jc. "A" Down Loop Home Signal).	951 yards Canterbury Jc. "A" side.
Down Loop Home Signal	150 yards Canterbury Jc. "A" side.
Down Main Home Signal	150 yards Chartham side.
Up Distant Signals (2) (beneath Canterbury West Up Platform Starting and Up Through Starting Signals).	673 yards Canterbury West side.
Up Main Home Signal (controlled by Canterbury West as Up Advanced Starting Signal).	106 yards Canterbury West side, situated on separate post on left hand side of existing Canterbury West Up Advanced Starting Signal (see next below).

CANTERBURY.

Bringing into use, and doubling of, the former Single Loop Line connecting the Line between Faversham and Canterbury East with the Line between Ashford and Canterbury West, together with the re-opening of Canterbury Junction "A" and "B" Signal Boxes, situated at each end of the Loop Line.

To be carried out on Sunday, 22nd February, commencing at 8.30 a.m.

CANTERBURY JUNCTION "A" BOX

Canterbury Jc. "A" Signal Box, situated on the Up Side between Canterbury East and Chartham Crossing, will be again brought into use.

The former Single Loop Line to Canterbury Jc. "B" will be brought into use as the Down Loop Line, the facing points in the Down Main Line, 190 yards Canterbury East side of Signal Box, which are at present clipped and padlocked in the normal position, being connected up and worked from the Signal Box. These Points will, in future, normally lie for the Down Loop Line.

The trap points in the Down Loop Line, 256 yards Canterbury Jc. "B" side of Signal Box, which are at present clipped and padlocked in the normal position, will, in future, be clipped and padlocked in the reverse position.

A new Up Loop Line from Canterbury Jc. "B" will be provided with trailing Points in the Up Main Line, 228 yards Canterbury East side of Signal Box. Self-acting Spring Catch Points will be provided in this Up Loop Line, 417 yards Canterbury Jc. "B" side of the Up Loop Home Signal, and a sand drag provided.

The existing Canterbury West Up Advanced Starting Signal, 106 yards Canterbury West side of Canterbury Jc. "B" Box, will, in future, apply as Canterbury Jc. "B" Up Loop Home Signal.

A new banner repeating Signal, consisting of a black arm, will be provided on the half-bracket post beneath Canterbury West Up Through Inner Home Signal, 463 yards the approach side of the Canterbury Jc. "B" Box Up Distant Signal. The new banner repeating Signal will work in conjunction with and repeat the position of the Up Distant Signal and will be illuminated at night.

A new banner repeating Signal, consisting of a black arm, will be provided on the overbridge 100 yards approach side of the Up Home Signals. The new banner repeating Signal will work in conjunction with the Up Main Home and Up Loop Home Signals, giving Drivers, etc. an indication as to whether both these Signals are in the normal position or either one is in the "clear" position, and will be illuminated at night.

The existing Canterbury West Down Main Distant Signal will, in future, apply as an outer Distant Signal and also as Canterbury Jc. "B" Down Main Distant Signal.

Canterbury Jc. "B" Down Loop Distant Signal will also apply as Canterbury West Down Loop outer Distant Signal.

The distances between the respective Distant and Home Signals are shown below :—

Between	Distance
Down Main Distant and Down Main Home	702 yards.
Down Loop Distant and Down Loop Home	801 yards.
Up Distants and Up Homes	567 yards.

CANTERBURY WEST.

New Down Inner Distant Signals will be provided beneath Canterbury Jc. "B" Down Main Home Signal and Down Loop Home Signal, and will each be 587 yards from the Down Home Signals.

The distances between the Down Main and Down Loop outer Distant Signals (see under "Canterbury Jc. 'B' Box") and the new Down Main and Down Loop Inner Distant Signals will then be 702 and 801 yards respectively.

(S.O.O. R.89900.)   (L.E.D. F.278.R, F.361.R.)   (P/EW, No. 8, L.E.D., 1953.)

This page - Canterbury Loop signalling notice and diagram, February / March 1953.

Opposite - *Two views of the reinstated Canterbury Loop recorded on 22 February 1953. In the top illustration to the right the line is to Canterbury East, the loop line curved around to join the line from Ashford - the route of the latter passing under the bridge just seen on the extreme right. The lower view is towards Canterbury Junction 'B' - indicated.*

After the line was restored on 21 May the M7s returned home and the former LCDR and SECR locomotives resumed normal duties.

Four additional push-pull sets were drafted in from other parts of the Southern Region, and returned once the crisis was over. Two ten-compartment trailers with push-pull through connections were also drafted in for strengthening proposes. On 21 May two ten-compartment thirds were returned from Herne Bay to Brockenhurst (S1098S) and Seaton (S1050S), and the 4 two-coach push-pull sets from Faversham each returned to Bexhill West, Ashford, Gravesend Central and Allhallows-on-Sea. Damage to the ferry terminal at Harwich, when the train ferry 'Essex' lifted and damaged the link span, threw the weight of cross-channel traffic on to the Dover to Dunkirk ferry until it was repaired.

Opposite top - Pull-Push set at Chestfield, 2 May 1953. 'M7' No. 30129 with set No. 714 reported as the 4.06 pm Faversham to Herne Bay service although seen with just a single pair of vehicles.   *Denis Cullum.*

Opposite bottom - An undated view at the same location, with this time the engine being sandwiched.

This page, top - Herne Bay, 'C' class 0-6-0 No. 31461 departing with the 5.34 pm to Faversham, 2 May 1953.

The Lens of Sutton Collection.

This page, bottom - Engineers construction camp, near MP69½ near Reculvers. The view was taken on 19 April 1953 facing towards Margate. The vehicles, all of which had their interiors removed and replaced with bunks, were Nos, 6541, 3163, 3104, 3312, 687 and 6487.

The Lens of Sutton Collection.

Top - *East from MP 67 showing the new chalk wall and Reculver's Up Distant.*

Left - *The diminutive Reculver Signal Box and associated Down and Up Home Signals. This signal box, more accurately described at a wooden GF hut, contained six levers and was in use by 1871. It was closed from 3 May 1959.*

Bottom - *The new chalk wall between Reculvers and Birchington. The towers accommodated floodlights. All, 19 April 1953.*

> *The Lens of Sutton Collection.*

Right - *The final poster, Waterloo (Eastern) 1 June 1953. Each of the posters were numbered in consecutive sequence as the work progressed.*

> *The Lens of Sutton Collection.*

Bottom - *Kearnsey Loop Junction.*

The cost of repairs, including the re-instatement of the Canterbury loops was in the order of £150,000. All the repair work to the railway installation was carried out by railway personnel withdrawn from normal maintenance, but certain ancillary work such as fencing was carried out by contractors.

The problems afflicting the Southern Region in the early part of 1953 were not at an end, however: on 24 April No. 35020 sustained a broken axle at speed at Crewkerne --- but that is another story!

Sources- Contemporary accounts in Railway Observer, Railway Magazine, Trains Illustrated, Southern Region Special Traffic Arrangements and Special Traffic Notices, Railway Executive report into effects of 1953 flood. Various newspaper accounts of the flood.

Views of trains on the Kearnsey loop as well as diversions and a spoil train in consequence of the engineering work will be found in our September title, *SOUTHERN REGION MEMORIES - PHOTOGRAPHS FROM THE BLUEBELL MUSEUM ARCHIVE*

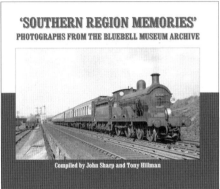

'SOUTHERN REGION MEMORIES'
PHOTOGRAPHS FROM THE BLUEBELL MUSEUM ARCHIVE

Compiled by John Sharp and Tony Hillman

BRITISH RAILWAYS

SPECIAL ANNOUNCEMENT

The repair of sea defences in the Thanet flood area is making rapid progress and direct train services from LONDON are

NOW IN OPERATION

to RAMSGATE, BROADSTAIRS, MARGATE, WESTGATE AND BIRCHINGTON via Faversham and Minster

to WHITSTABLE AND HERNE BAY (changing at Faversham)

with connecting bus services to BIRCHINGTON AND WESTGATE

and the SITTINGBOURNE – QUEENBOROUGH – SHEERNESS service

ALL SERVICES WILL BE RESTORED TO NORMAL ON THURSDAY. 21st MAY

Permanent Way Notes by Graham Hatton
Borough Market Junction, London Bridge

Borough Market lies in the shadow of Southwark Cathedral and this is a rare wartime photograph taken in 1942. The photograph, which is undoubtedly taken from the signal box controlling the exceptionally busy junction, shows the two lines diverging to Waterloo East and Charing Cross towards the top with four lines from Cannon Street to the right (opened in Jan 1864) and onwards to London Bridge at the bottom. The signal box here closed on 16 April 1976. The route has always been busy with some unique operating practices to get train 'headways' (the distance between trains) to the absolute minimum. Since 1991, Borough Market Junction has just been a gathering of lines here, as all the pointwork associated with the diverging routes is at the other end of the station. The two lines to Waterloo East are now sometimes known as 'The Critical' from here to Metropolitan Junction, about a quarter of a mile further on, on that route, and where the route becomes four tracks again. A further group of tracks leave these four lines at that point to form part of the current Thameslink route through Blackfriars. The actual Market lies immediately below the diverging routes, the line to Waterloo crossing over the Market roof!

So critical is this section of line that this is at last being relieved by a further two lines being built through from London Bridge to Metropolitan Junction on a brand new viaduct and on to link into the Thameslink route. Some of the buildings on the left in this picture, and still standing, are being demolished to allow this to happen, whilst retaining Borough Market below it all. There is a further side to the triangle from Cannon Street to Waterloo East (opened between Cannon Street South and West Junctions in June 1878) which has supported various services over the years, but is now largely for stock movements. Thus a very crowded part of London both at this level and below it!

Of permanent way note here is that a number of these crossings are full depth castings fishplated to adjacent Bullhead track. The castings are directly screwed to the timbers by pairs of screws through the flat-bottom-style foot to the castings.

The lines are all electrified, but due to the complex track arrangement there is a significant gap in the feeding arrangements through the junction itself. Trains would bridge this gap with collector shoes spaced along the train and commoned together electrically, or simply coast a short distance without power.

Right - If there was a list of junctions which saw a lot of relaying and renewal of components, then Borough Market would feature heavily in this list. Despite war-time shortages, this photograph taken in October 1944 illustrates that renewal had clearly become essential. This is a view from the 'vee' of the junction with the signal box on the left and the lines to Waterloo East on the right, and shows the lines reducing from the four coming from London Bridge station in the distance (originally three and widened on the right to four in 1902) to two to Waterloo East in the centre right foreground and four continuing to Cannon Street on the left of the foreground. This is a slightly later picture in the renewal process, but illustrates the junction well and the piecemeal nature of renewal at this stage. Only enough ballast to allow timber renewal has been opened out and in this case would have been loaded on to a train, by hand. There is no room to put

ballast on the side for re-use here. The bigger nature of the castings is clearly illustrated, as are the paint markings on the bottom left hand rails to assist in positioning them when re-installed here. These would have been painted on when the layout was built up from all the various separate items, known as pre-assembly, which it is believed took place at New Cross Yard for this item.

Layouts would probably have been direct rebuilds of earlier designs at this time. For construction reasons you have to have something to work from, and the line of survey pegs would give a good straight line (marked on the drawing as well) to measure from as required. The technical office staff would have also marked critical dimensions on any adjacent item along with the Supervisor, 'just to be on the safe side!' This is a tradition which still happens today. Consequent upon the closure of the signal box at Borough Market Junction on 19 April 1976, it was removed in one piece and now resides at the National Railway Museum in York complete with contents. Although not officially open yet, the wooden operating floor is at ground level, so it is possible to peer in the window and view the original diagram and equipment including the train selection method of communication.					(Caption to below view overleaf.)

Previous page, bottom - A later date but also believed to be a picture of Switches & Crossings (S & C) for Borough Market. This photograph is being used to illustrate assembly of the new S & C prior to despatch to the site. Life expectancy of this junction could be in single figures of years, but in that time it saw far more trains than most other much-longer-lived junctions away from London. So it is no surprise to see this layout being renewed again in this photograph taken in February 1954, in New Cross Yard. Of note are the loose components coming together to form the layout before it was all marked in paint and carefully dismantled to travel to site loose or in large assemblies of components as far as possible, which sometimes exceeded the normal loading gauge. In that case these assemblies were restricted by physical limitations en route to the site and the limit of loading on wagons and could overhang the wagon sides by a considerable amount. They would move to site when other lines were closed and the load would be carefully transferred with an appropriate out-of-gauge supervisor. P/Way Supervisors could be quite 'imaginative' about loading wagons when circumstances allowed! The line of survey pegs is again evident. This line was replicated in the depot and on site and used to reassemble the layout from a known point. Drawings of Switch and Crossing layouts of this complexity were drawn to scales often much larger than the common 1:48 (now 1:50) as used on simpler layouts, to allow the detail to show. However the men putting the layout together had a huge amount of experience in assembling complex layouts, which the railways specialised in at this time, and would understand the 'order of construction' to achieve completion. Many items being specially made in the 'diamond area' would be very rigid, so after laying critical crossings and following one rail throughout on the timbers, using offsets from the pegged straight line to achieve the desired shape of that track, the second rail would be gauged from this. The critical elements, crossings and then switches go in first and the layout is built outwards in a layout like this to the loose ends where, on site, it will be 'cut in' to the existing track. Layouts are still built in much the same way. A small steam crane would assist assembly, but this is still hard physical work!

Above - Back in 1944 and the junction is slowly coming together. The timbers of the portion in the foreground would probably have been despatched loose in a wagon for spacing on site, the chairs would have remained attached after they were fitted in the pre-assembly area. However the deep castings of the many crossings would have been unscrewed and then re-fixed, this time with the screws fully tightened. The back of an engineer's train loaded with components lies on the down Waterloo East line.

Right - Just to illustrate the use of the steam crane for moving items about. There are a lot of people in a small space here, but it is obvious who is senior by the trilby hats, as opposed to the vast numbers of flat caps! The manual augers, 'T' spanners and keying hammer would have been familiar to railway workers 60 years earlier, and are still familiar to them today as back up tools to motorised versions which achieve exactly the same task, but with a lot less effort. A report of this relaying also appeared on page 109 of the SR Magazine for Nov / Dec 1944 with the following notes, " When previously renewed in 1932 full advantage was taken to provide the best possible alignment having regard to the space available. Since 1932 it has been necessary to change the crossing rails more than once because of excessive wear, even though the previous junction (which was designed to standard built-up practice) incorporated 95lb. per yard high manganese steel rails. The new layout was built by a Sheffield contractor but before it was placed in the track it was assembled and checked for alignment and gauge on its new timbers at a layout ground at New Cross Gate. In order to keep a certain number of lines open to traffic during the renewal of the junction and to provide facilities for the operation of cranes and material trains, the work was carried out on three successive Sundays and traffic was worked to Waterloo and Charing Cross via Cannon Street when the direct roads were unusable."

Left - The layout is almost complete and time for a pause for thought! The junction between the full depth castings and the adjacent BH rail is illustrated on the left. Various chairs are visible and on the right of the track in the foreground are slab and bracket chairs with long bolts passing through the brackets, rails and spacing blocks resting on a large flat plate (the slab). In the four-foot lies a 'T' spanner, a tool still in use today. It was used between two men alternating hands on the top bar to drive in chair-screws; similar items were used for smaller screws such as conductor rail pot screws. A day using this was not the most rewarding job and would guarantee blisters for anyone whose hands were not already as hard as leather!

Opposite, bottom - Of interest to those who follow signalling. It is not believed there was ever a long term ground frame at this location, as shunting did not take place here. It seems likely that in order to facilitate the work, and maybe as a result of the work being completed in stages, which required disconnecting of the mechanical rodding between the various stages, a temporary ground frame was used. This is further evidenced by the fact that the levers in the frame are numbered 3, 17 and 26 which presumably were their normal signal box frame numbers, rather than being numbered 1 to 3 etc. as would be normal in a ground frame. The points appear motor-operated, but mechanically connected to the frame in some form, so how the system worked is unknown, but the levers appear to work 'point' from the plate descriptions and they may not have been interlocked in the normal way if they were a very short term arrangement. The coat on the frame doubtless belonged to a 'person in authority.' It would appear some trains were running as two of the men in the foreground appear to be lookouts or hand-signalmen. **This page, top -** Although taken in 1960 these two pictures are of life below the relentless movement of trains and the battle to maintain the railway for their operation. The sheer diversity of the baskets and crates is of interest in this typical market scene which could almost be any market but is labelled on the reverse as Borough Market and which clearly lies below the arches and columns supporting the railway. Alfred Shread Ltd. appears to be selling Jaffa oranges in the crates in the middle. You can almost here the market noise of the process of selling in a best South London accent. **Right -** This photograph shows the same owner's pitch, with bananas in the foreground, and possibly boxes of apples and bags of potatoes. Above and around lies the ever present railway. At the time these photographs were taken the service through here saw peaks of about 100 trains an hour, 1000 per day. Today it is often cited as the busiest place on British Railways, and to increase the available paths for trains towards Waterloo East and Thameslink services a new viaduct is being constructed along with station alterations at all the neighbouring stations to allow even greater numbers of trains to flow through this area.

'REBUILT'-THE LETTERS AND COMMENTS PAGE(S)

That man Rod Garner - he of 'Torrington & Marland' and more recent 'Bideford. Westward Ho! & Appledore' writings*, contacted us recently with an unusual query passed to him by a local resident. Apparently In 1901, The Bideford, Westward Ho and Appledore Railway had a tariff which included a charge of 2/6 for the carriage of a harp: "...in or out of its case." Was this peculiar to the BWHA or standard practice on the LSWR and even elsewhere? The thought so far is that the charge may have been invented to cover a specific, perhaps local, need, maybe even applicable to just a single occasion. Does any learned reader have any thoughts.

Any responses to the Editor or even direct to Rod at:

rodgarner@tiscali.co.uk

* both available from Kestrel Railway Books.

We have a few areas to cover this month, some relative to recent issues and some from slightly further back, likewise from previous and new contributors. Starting then on Crawley from Gordon Gravett - Gordon it will be recalled afforded much of the local information for the photographic feature on the station as appeared in issue 11. "One small point that I may have missed in the draft you sent me is that there was not a level crossing at Southgate Avenue. That was a new road in the 1950s to the new housing estates at Southgate and Tilgate and passed under the railway to the east of the station, just beyond the goods yard. The two level crossings were the High Street / Brighton Road crossing (it was High Street north of the railway and Brighton Road to the south) and the one you mention at Horsham Road - about 500 yards west of the station."

Then from Viv Orchard again reference Issue No. 11. "The superb picture at Ventnor West on pages 30 / 31 questions whether this is Set 483 or 484. A good friend states it is Set 483. The Driving coach of Set 483 had a saloon window half way along and the panelling by the Guards door was sheeted over. Neither of these existed on Set 484. Set 484 has been beautifully restored and is running on the Isle of Wight Railway. The very

interesting article on Signalling Schools will I am sure produce further facts. There were two regimes for the schools. The Operating function was concerned with the Rules and Regulations for signalmen and others. The Signal & Telegraph Department were concerned with the training of staff who had to maintain the equipment. Such facilities were also used to test new equipment, such as the point machines for Feltham Marshalling Yard. The S & T School at Wimbledon also eventually moved to Clapham Junction but at the Windsor end of the Yard. Later, as Resources Engineer for the South Western Division, I was charged with establishing a new Training School at Woking together with an outside track layout and its associated equipment. The Old Relay Room at Waterloo was adopted as a training facility as was the old Wimbledon 'A' signal box for its mechanical equipment. Similar S & T training establishments were created at Purley and on the South Eastern Division. I am trying to ascertain more detail on these establishments. As an aside, many years ago, when a contractor installed a new installation, apprentices produced miniature lever frames complete with interlocking for presentation to the Chief of the day. One wonders where those frames went to?"

On different tack now from Mr. P Hotchin, "I enclose a scan of a photograph in my collection which I think you will find of interest. Taken at Victoria in 1937 it depicts one of the special buses used by London transport to operate the inter-station service. They were painted in a Blue and Cream livery with the words 'INTER-STATION' on the side and accommodated a large luggage boot under the half-deck. The same layout was later adopted for Airport coaches. The service was a useful facility linking the main line stations for whilst most of the London stations were served by the Underground network this latter system could be tiresome if a passenger had a lot of luggage, particularly if a change of train was required."

We have received the following from one of regular contributors to these pages subsequent to reading No. 11, " The attached is totally spontaneous. There is another Winchester tale which I doubt is for publication (- oh yes it is!), but told as things were 60 years ago in my world. At Oxford, the last weekend before Finals in June was known as Schools Weekend, when we were all meant to get the hell out and forget it all.

"After various ideas had been censured, it was agreed that I should spend the weekend with my then girlfriend in Bournemouth and I would meet her at Winchester station and drive to Bournemouth, no doubt lingering in the New Forest. So I took my beloved Morris Minor to Winchester and about 6 pm stood on the up platform waiting for the arrival of bliss. What happened was that the tannoy suddenly woke up and said, very carefully and distinctly, If Mr...............is on the platform waiting to meet Miss......travelling from Bournemouth, please would he come to the Parcels Office on the down platform.

"So he did, she'd missed the train, so I drove alone. No she hadn't dumped me: that was two months later."

From the same source comes this story, "In April 1957 I had an official footplate pass for a trip from Waterloo to Bournemouth Central and return. Inspector Plummer was detailed to travel with me, as he had done for other trips. We had 'Standard 5' No. 73115 on the down run and when we reached Bournemouth I commented that I was rattled to pieces and nearly deaf. The Inspector said I thought you had asked for a Standard or I would have got it changed. I assured him that I had not made the choice, so saying he would see about it and that he had some business to attend to, he finished by adding we would travel together from Southampton Central.

"I accepted this because I thought he must have some reason for the change and so made my own way back on another service to 'central. Thus in due course we met at the London end of the Up Fast platform, (Platform 1) at Southampton. The train on which I was to ride was signalled and when it appeared it was with No. 34031 'Torrington' at the head. The Inspector burst out laughing when he saw my face, he had guessed correctly this is exactly what I would have chosen.

We climbed aboard, the Inspector stood looking out of the Fireman's window and I stood behind the driver. We started off slowly through the tunnel and over the junction (Northam)

and then began to pick up speed. Somewhere after Swaythling when the Driver was satisfied with progress he got off his seat saying, You take her now, and crossed the cab to talk to the Inspector.

"That was a considerable surprise but a great opportunity, how could I refuse? So we forged ahead. I altered the cut off slightly and made sure the whistle was blown at every opportunity. The tricky bit was fast approaching as we were due to stop at Winchester. Any amateur steam driver will tell you that going is easy but stopping is horribly difficult. Winchester station is on the 1 in 252 climb which extends from Eastleigh to Litchfield Tunnel so there were conflicting forces to contend with. Fortunately I was given help and the instruction to Keep the van on the platform. This referred to a Southern utility van coupled behind the tender.

"The combination of professional and amateur did not quite succeed, as the front door of the van was over the platform ramp. The reason became apparent. A Company of The Rifle Brigade was travelling to London and the designed process was that the Riflemen entered the van by one door, deposited their kit, and left by the other door thus ensuring speedy loading and no delay. Unfortunately they only had one door available.

"There wasn't too much chaos, I suspect due to the NCOs present, and I am sure any delay was booked to the Locomotive Department. It did mean there was time to make up.

"Somehow I got away without slipping and tried to get moving as quickly as possible. Details are hazy after all these years, but I do remember passing Micheldever at what seemed a very reasonable speed and of course the obligatory whistling. Sadly I had to hand over before Worting Junction. Oddly I never found out the Driver's name. But I expect that somehow it was organised by the Inspector for a completely memorable day out."

Long overdue for publication is a letter from David Cockman who contacted us concerning his grandfather, James Cockman, the Paint Shop Foreman at Eastleigh from around 1945 until he retired in 1952. David writes, "I have a very early memory of grandfather which may be of interest. One Sunday he took me with him into the Carriage Works because he had an urgent job to complete. Just outside his little office, resting on two trestles, were two long and very large arrows. Granpa's job that day was to cover the arrows in sheet after sheet of gold leaf which he had in lots of books. The arrows were, of course, being made ready to fix to the side of the Bulleid pacific which was about to pull the inaugural post-war service of the Golden Arrow from London to Dover. I remember being astonished when Grandpa told me how much these books of gold leaf cost and how careful he had to be. I remain astonished, especially when you consider the austere living conditions and shortages of the 1940s. Why such extravagance, why not use just yellow paint, would anyone have been able to tell the difference? Still, whenever I come across an archive picture of the Golden Arrow on its way to Dover, I think of my own small part in its history. And I wonder where the arrows are now?"

David continues but adds, "There is one memory of my railway childhood that still makes me blush. This is the way in which workers in both the Carriage and Loco

David Cockman also submitted this staff view of 'Southern Railway Carriage & Wagon Works, Eastleigh', unfortunately undated.

We have no names so even allowing for space constraints in reproducing it at this size, if any-one is recognised we would be very pleased to hear the details.

Works 'borrowed' material on a grand scale form the Southern Railway. Perhaps it was regarded almost as perk of the job? Our somewhat rickety old house in Bishopstoke was virtually held together and maintained by these borrowed materials. Grandpa was always painting the house and shed. Which was fine as long as you liked SR green, since that was the only colour available. Likewise, inside the house all wooden surfaces and doors were finished in dark SR varnish, just like the inside of the coaches being built in the Works. In about 1948 Gramps decided what we needed some new clothes posts for the garden, which soon duly arrived from the Works, five long poles with beautifully turned hardwood pulleys and a well engineered mechanism for raising and lowering the clothes lines. The top of each pole carried a finial similar to that at the top of SR semaphore signal posts. They were still working when my mother died in 1999. On an-other occasion a set of hand made best SR leather cushions stuffed with best SR horse hair arrived for the garden benches. These lasted for at least two decades. My uncle Fred was an elec-trician in the Loco Works, but was always available for a bit of extra wiring, material provided as usual by 'don't ask' etc. etc. Of course the Works in those days was staffed by real craftsmen of every description who could turn their hands to whatever was required. It is something of a mystery how they actually found

time to build locos and carriages! Better stop, in case I get ar-rested for being an accessory....!"

David continues, " My grandfather and my father Wil-liam, between them gave just over a hundred years service on the railway at Eastleigh, father in both the locomotive and carriage works. Most relatives and neighbours were likewise employed on the railway, which dominated the life of the community during my childhood at Bishopstoke in the forties and fifties. (You could always tell where the engine drivers lived: their door knockers were tied up with a thick wadge of old socks or cloths to try and prevent their sleep being disturbed during the day when on a night turn."

"Between 1951 and 1959 the railway also played an important part in my daily routine, for I used to catch the train to go to Winchester where I was a pupil at Peter Symonds School. I still remember that routine quite clearly; in the mornings the 8.20 am to Winchester, and at tea time the 4.25 pm back home to Eas-tleigh, (at least before the Hampshire dieselisation scheme.) I mention this because on Page 11 in your book 'The Heyday of Eastleigh and its Locomotives - Ian Allan') you refer to the crip-pled driver of the B4 at Winchester. I remember him well; his name was , I think, Frank, and he also would catch the 4.25 pm home and a group of us keen loco spotters would always try and

David Taylor, whose wonderful view of Coulsdon North appeared as the double page spread at the start of Issue 11, has also contributed this image of the 'Belle' circa 1937. We suspect in the Redhill area.

sit with him for a chat about trains. From some of the upstairs class rooms at Peter Symonds there was a good view down onto the yard at Winchester and we would while away many a boring lesson watching the B4 buzz up and down. I don't think Frank used, to do much except sit peacefully on the footplate while the fireman did all that was required, it seemed to us then the most idyllic job in the world. Incidentally, the 8.20 am service in the morning would bring up the carriages for the 4.25 pm service. It would leave Winchester station, back into the yard, detach the two carriages and then wait for the fast London service to depart ahead of it, before pulling out and continuing on its way to Reading. I often wondered what passengers made of this rather unusual movement. Did they feel abandoned as they waited in the sidings?

"You also mention the boat trains from Southampton. These were particularly welcome to the big gang of reluctant pupils on the 8.20 am, for if the timings were right, we could manage to miss the first lesson of the day. The first good omen was the 8.20 am being held at the signal south of Shawford. We waited, listening out for the Bulleid or 'Nelson' as it pulled the heavy boat trams uphill towards Winchester. If it passed and we still waited, this was more good news, for it meant a second one following in quick succession. And then an extra delay was possible as the 8.20 am was held back further so that the scheduled London fast service would not be blocked. Another ruse for arriving late at school was to catch the Great Western Service from Eastleigh at around 8.am. This was going to Newbury and Didcot via Winchester Chesil, which meant a long slow walk across Winchester to Peter Symonds."

Keith Hastie has kindly forwarded a copy of an LSW pocket timetable for the summer of 1914 covering the Ringwood to Christchurch line. (See SW No 4) He writes, "I don't know what prompted me to send you a copy of the enclosed leaflet, but I think it would be of interest if nothing else. the Bournemouth & District MRC had club rooms in the old Parcels Office (now demolished) at Branksome station and in the process of cleaning out the office we came across lots of leaflets etc. under a hatch in the floor. A railway version of sweeping things under the carpet!"

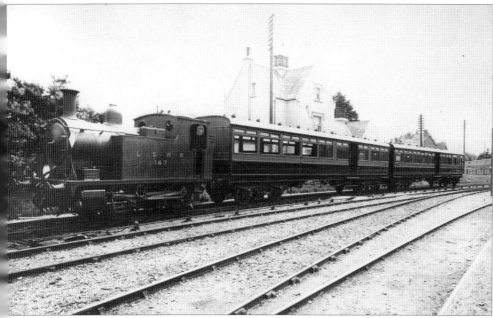

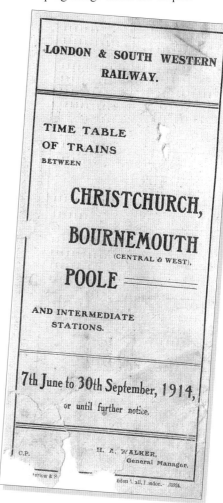

LONDON & SOUTH WESTERN RAILWAY.

TIME TABLE OF TRAINS BETWEEN

CHRISTCHURCH, BOURNEMOUTH (CENTRAL & WEST), POOLE

AND INTERMEDIATE STATIONS.

7th June to 30th September, 1914, or until further notice.

J. C.P.   H. A. WALKER, General Manager.

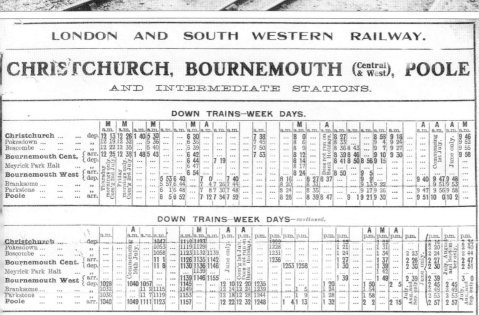

LONDON AND SOUTH WESTERN RAILWAY.

CHRISTCHURCH, BOURNEMOUTH (Central & West), POOLE AND INTERMEDIATE STATIONS.

DOWN TRAINS—WEEK DAYS.

This page, top left - Up Motor train at Christchurch (old) station before heading north to Ringwood.

Bottom left - One page of the aforementioned timetable. 'M' indicates 'Motor' 'A' indicates 1st and 2nd class only.

Terry Cole's Rolling Stock File No. 13

Strengthening Vehicles

The Southern ran most of its trains with fixed formation sets so at times of peak demand it had need of additional vehicles to increase train capacity. In this 'File' we look at 3 different designs of vehicle often used for this purpose.

Opposite top - This coach, S194S, started life in November 1898 as LSWR 48ft 8-compartment Third 88, one of several hundred such vehicles built from 1894 onwards. In the 1930s the Southern Railway set about 'modernising' these coaches and many were rebuilt for the 'new' electric trains. However 38 were rebuilt as steam stock coaches. This vehicle, now 194, was rebuilt in April 1935 on to a new 58ft underframe with an extra compartment and two lavatories to become a 9-compartment lav-third to diagram 31. Used predominately as a 'loose' coach on the Western section, it was withdrawn in August 1959 and is seen here in the sidings at Horsted Keynes after withdrawal. You can see the dreaded X within a circle at the near end denoting a condemned vehicle. A similar vehicle, No. S320S, was one of the two original coaches purchased by the Bluebell Railway but unfortunately it has been out of use waiting major rebuilding for several years.

Opposite bottom - Here we see ex SECR 10-compartment third S974S built at Ashford in 1923 Originally SECR No 1437, it was one of 66 vehicles built to a similar design. Initially most of these vehicles were used more or less permanently to augment semi-fast and excursion trains where their 100 seating capacity was a boon to the operating department. With their hard narrow bench seats, travelling very far in them was however distinctly uncomfortable. By the 1950s many had become 'loose' coaches and could be found almost anywhere on the system, witness this one at Sidmouth on 26 August 1959 ready to be added to a train at a moments notice. The Bluebell Railway purchased two of these vehicles in 1963 including sister coach No. 971 whilst their solid construction has meant that they have been in traffic much of the time since.

This page - Corridor trains needed strengthening too and for this Maunsell designed the open third coach. S1314S seen here at Padstow on 27 August 1962, one of 50 such vehicles built in 1932/3 to Diagram 2005 An unusual feature is that the whole 'picture' window can be slid downwards, giving rise to the name 'Drop window Thirds.' Twenty were modified from 1959 as trailer coaches for the 'new' Maunsell Push-Pull sets but No. 1314 was not one of these and it was withdrawn in November 1962. The Bluebell Railway has an example in traffic so its comforts can be experienced first hand.

(All photos David Wigley)

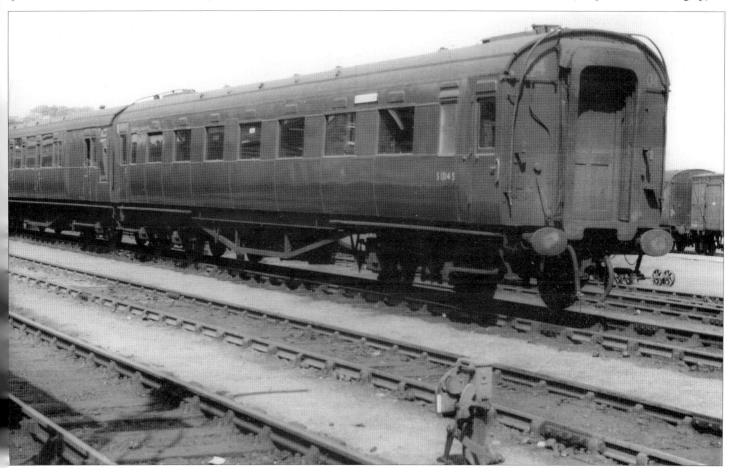

Top - *Streatham Common Shunting Box following the attentions of a Zeppelin raid during WW1. This sort of damage was easily fixed as it was in this case, the building serving for another sixty years or so, surviving the signalling upgrade of the early 1950s as a Ground Frame finally succumbing to the Victoria resignalling scheme of the 1980s.*

Bottom - *Charing Cross Signal Box, this is the new power signal box mentioned in the text. The layout prior to the alterations for the 10-car train scheme of the late fifties is clearly shown, including the short storage sidings on the Eastern section of the bridge. The date of the picture is not known but it was most likely taken in the late 20s or early 30s.*

The SOUTHERN RAILWAY:
from Inception, through to Nationalisation and beyond.
Part 3 - The Prioities
Tony Goodyear

(Previous instalments in this series appeared in Issues 6 & 8.)

When new organisations first take up office it is rare that they hit the ground running and despite their best efforts this was particularly the case with the management structure when the new Southern Railway organisation took office on 1 January 1923. Earlier in this series we looked at some of the specific preparations that were put in place to keep the day to day operations going prior to the new organisation taking over, in an attempt at minimising the confusion and lack of direction that often accompanies these momentous events. In part 3 - The Priorities, we cover the actions and events of the first two years or so of the Southern Railway's existence. For the sake of completeness I have also finished the story off in individual cases.

On formation, the Southern Railway found itself with what amounted to three Southern Railways, separately managed by three 'Superintendents of the Line'. Sir Herbert Walker proposed, to the board, a new organisation based on a departmental structure, which was introduced 1 January 1924, a full year after the formation of the new company.

Under Walker's plan the organisation was split into Operating and Commercial departments, formed into six divisions below a 'Headquarters' organisation. The six Divisions were initially listed as follows: **London West** based on London Waterloo, which covered the old L&SWR suburban area from Waterloo and the main lines to both Southampton (as far as Basingstoke) and Portsmouth (as far as Havant), **London East** based on London Bridge and covering most of the old SE&CR suburban area and the LB&SCR suburban area, **Eastern** based on Ashford (later Dover) taking in the old SE&CR outside the London suburban area except Tonbridge Wells to Hastings, **Southern** based on Brighton taking in the LB&SCR outside the suburban area and the SE&CR line from Tonbridge Wells to Hastings, **Central** based on Southampton covering the L&SWR main line from Basingstoke (Worting Junc.) to Salisbury inc. the Bournemouth line from Basingstoke (Worting Junc.) to Bournemouth and on to Dorchester both via Poole and the old road (Castleman's Corkscrew) together with the branches, **Western** based on Exeter which covered the old L&SWR west of Salisbury together with the branches.

The arrangements outlined above were considerably altered in 1930 as part of a major reorganisation, of which more anon. The Somerset and Dorset line had its own separate management structure until 1 July 1930 and the Isle of Wight had an Assistant Divisional Operating Superintendent reporting via the London West divisional organisation.

At the same time (1924) a new engineering organisation was also put in place. This had seven districts. Needless to say the boundaries of these districts did not exactly line up with those of the operating divisions, again requiring some tidying up in latter years.

It was early in 1924 that, at long last, the Southern was able to make real decisions about its future direction. In reality the Southern got off lightly, as the LMS was still suffering from the sparring about policy between the factions at Derby and Crewe some ten years after its formation, and the LNER was not immune from such problems either. The first priority for the new Southern team was to start sorting out the unfinished works and orders originally put in hand by the old companies, together with the problems and dilemmas faced in completing them. In those days, just as on the modern privatised railway, ongoing works generally had to continue and commitments to contractors had to be honoured.

The Southern, along with the LMS and LNER, inherited a number of individual ongoing projects from its constituent companies, the GWR being lucky and mostly just carrying on as before; it was only in the Valleys and on the Cambrian that immediate action was needed. Occasionally, when it was no longer relevant or prudent to proceed with work previously authorised by the absorbed company, a project would be cancelled. It should also be remembered that cancelling a project, when it is already underway, can create more problems than it solves, particularly where contracts for the supply of materials or construction of the work have already been entered into. The case of the completion of the LB&SCR suburban electrification is dealt with below.

Urgent amongst the outstanding work was the completion of the ongoing war repairs. This project, or more correctly

group of projects, was, in theory at least, paid for by the government, and was designed to return the railway to the condition it was when war was declared at midnight on 4 August 1914. The main thrust of the work was eliminating the backlog of maintenance, particularly the replacement of worn-out track and point-work, in order to permit the lifting of the numerous temporary speed restrictions that had been imposed as the track condition deteriorated during the war. Additionally there was a huge quantity of bridges, culverts, drains, ditches and fences that needed to be brought up to standard, along with the cutting back of undergrowth and trees along the right of way. This situation arose as a result of the government taking control of the railways when war was declared, which was quickly followed by many of the younger members of staff, particularly those engaged on Permanent Way work, volunteering and joining the forces, leaving a staff shortage.

Towards the end of 1916 the level of non-military passenger and goods traffic carried by the railways had risen to record levels. After making some allowance for the transport of essential workers, the 'Railway Executive Committee' (REC) considered that there was an element of 'joy-riding'. Given the need to provide additional locomotives and materials for the war effort, the REC submitted a memorandum to the Board of Trade detailing the action required to curtail unnecessary travel. The proposals were divided into those that required government action for implementation and those that did not. The proposals included: passenger train services to be considerably reduced (in order to release locomotives); fares to be substantially increased (by 50%); certain branch and secondary lines to be closed (the story of the Basingstoke and Alton is recounted below); the practice of running mixed trains to be extended; express trains to be decelerated; reduction of leave to all branches of HM Forces serving in this country; reduction of Sunday trains; and limitation on the amount of free luggage. Following an order- in-council the additional restrictions were implemented on 1 January 1917

With the reduction of train speeds, which was intended to release locomotives for the war effort, it also effectively permitted a reduction in the standards of maintenance that could be tolerated. In fact, over the four years of war, little other than essential maintenance was carried out and only new work directly associated with the war effort was authorised.

Just to add to the difficulties, on 4 October 1916, and as a direct contribution to the war effort, the REC, of which H A Walker was acting Chairman, wrote to all the main railway companies asking them to provide second-hand permanent way materials, which were in short supply, to the war department. The initial enquiry was less than successful and it was followed up, in the December, with the demands requiring the railway companies to reduce services, increase fares and provide (collectively) 200 miles of second-hand materials for the war effort. The REC provided each company with a quota that it was required to fulfil and the L&SWR was asked for twelve miles. With unbelievable haste the L&SWR sacrificed the Basingstoke and Alton light railway, which had opened as recently as the first of June 1901 but was running at a loss. The public were given just one week's notice of the 'temporary' closure of the line which took effect on 30 January 1917.

Scenes from the film 'The Wrecker'. From top to bottom: The SR F1 4-4-0 on its side following the staged crash, Benita Hume grabbing the rear hand rail of what looks like a 'Thanet' Brake Third, Joseph Striker clambering over the tender of a U class locomotive (probably A803) to warn the crew to stop the train, a narrow escape! as an open top car races the train to an open crossing (you would get at least 6 points on your licence for this these days).

Following the cessation of hostilities the L&SWR took no action in restoring the line; just two short stubs were then in use, one at each end, for goods traffic. When the Southern Railway took office they decided to seek powers to abandon the Basingstoke and Alton light railway altogether, on the basis that it did not pay. Accordingly they introduced a bill in the 1923 session of Parliament. Following some wrangling in both Houses of Parliament the bill was withdrawn on the understanding that the line would be reinstated, and the situation reviewed again after ten years. Not everything went according to plan though. The line was rebuilt and reopened on 16 August 1924. However, just eight years later at 7.30 pm on 10 September 1932 the last passenger train left Alton for Basingstoke. Goods trains continued to run, over parts of the line until 31 May 1936.

During the last of its two short lives as a railway this little line acquired another claim to fame, or perhaps it was two, for in 1928 the Gainsborough Pictures film 'The Wrecker' was filmed at Salter Hatch Crossing near Lasham. The Southern did very well out this particular film contract by selling the film company a life-expired 'F1' class 4-4-0, No. A148 and six ex-SER bogie carriages, similar to those on the Isle of Wight, and they then got paid to clear up the mess after the filming. After the line was closed in 1936, track lifting got underway in 1937 but fate soon dealt a different hand when Gainsborough Pictures approached the Southern again for the use of a branch line for the making of what became the all-time classic

Herriard Park,
Basingstoke.
22nd December, 1922.

Dear Sir,

BASINGSTOKE & ALTON LIGHT RAILWAY.

As you are probably aware the London & South Western Railway Company are bringing an Omnibus Bill before the House of Commons for powers to, among other items, abandon the Basingstoke and Alton Light Railway.

The Mayor of Basingstoke is arranging a Meeting of Protest to be held at the Town Hall, Basingstoke, at 3 p.m. on Wednesday, 10th January, 1923 (should the date be altered I will let you know), at which our Member, Sir Arthur Holbrook, will be present.

May I ask you to make a special effort to be present at this Meeting to support the protest, as it is of vital importance that the abandonment of the line be opposed.

I intend, in conjunction with my neighbouring Landowners and others interested, to do all that is possible to have this line re-opened.

Yours faithfully,

F. H. T. JERVOISE.

Top - *Notice of an open meeting at Basingstoke Town Hall to oppose the Parliamentary Bill being promoted by the L&SWR to abandon the Basingstoke & Alton Light Railway.*

Bottom - *Ready to leave Victoria for Coulsdon North is a ten vehicle train of ex LB&SCR overhead stock, taken during the last week of operation, the power cars (Milk Vans) are the third and the eighth vehicles, which equates to two five car trains with a centre power car coupled together (there was no passenger accommodation in the power cars).*

Above - Norwood Junction looking South in Brighton Overhead days, during an incredibly quiet period as nothing appears to be moving and only one movement is signalled (on the Up Relief as it was called then).
Opposite - Electrical Engineers Report on future Electrification.

'Oh Mr Porter'. Again the Southern did well out of the contract with the hire of X6 4-4-0 No. 657 and an 0395 0-6-0 for the goods trains, together with the provision of crews and other rolling stock as required; an unexpected "nice little earner". Another oddity was the use of Kent and East Sussex Railway 2-4-0T 'Northiam', suitably renamed, as a co-star. (See also 'The Southern and the Silver Screen': Issue No. 7 of 'SW'.)

As well as putting the line in order and having to relay an unwanted branch line, there was the issue of the upgrading works on the old SE&CR lines. Further work on improving the line came to an end for the duration of the war, after completion of part of the upgrade of the Chatham main line which had allowed the increase of axle loadings to 19¼ tons in 1914. C F Dendy Marshall reports that at the Southern Railway Annual General Meeting (AGM) in February 1925 the chairman, General Baring, stated that even after the SE&CR had spent considerable sums of money on upgrading works, the Southern Railway had to allocate a further £250,000 to strengthen the bridges on the Eastern Section sufficiently to carry any type of engine used by the Southern Railway.

The following year, on the 25 February 1926, he returned to the subject, stating that of the three boat train routes between Victoria, Folkestone and Dover, boat train route one via Tonbridge and Folkestone was already available for use by 'King Arthur' class locomotives. Boat train route two via Swanley and Maidstone would be available by the end of March, and boat train route three via Chatham would be available for the summer traffic of the following year 1927, and that on that particular line it was the capabilities of the bridges over the river Medway that dictated the weight of locomotives that could be used. In fact it was to be the 19 June 1927, when the three-span bridge over the Medway was renewed, before any further weight restrictions on the Chatham section were removed.

Given the expenditure incurred by the SE&CR on upgrading its lines the Southern could reasonably have expected to have inherited a first-rate line but it still needed more investment to make it fit for the new owner's purposes. By way of preparing his shareholders for the bad news, General Baring pointed out to his audience that the bridges on the various sections were only constructed to carry the weight of the locos envisaged at the time they were built, and that very few routes were able to carry the weight of the new engines then being built.

Clearly, looking back at the events of well over ninety years ago, it is easy to see that the upgrade work then being carried out by the old SE&CR fell woefully short of what would be needed by the Southern. In this case it appears that the plans themselves were upgraded sufficiently by the new team to meet the revised remit. Regrettably this was not an isolated problem as some bridges on the Victoria to Newhaven route also needed strengthening, as well as clearance works to enable the 'King Arthurs' to work to Brighton and Eastbourne. C F Dendy Marshall's reports of the chairman's remarks at the early AGMs (1925/6/7) clearly conveys the irritation that the Board must have felt with having to put all manner of things in order before it could get on with the business of completing the Southern's inherited suburban electrification schemes.

The Southern had particular difficulties with its two uncompleted electrification schemes. As we saw in Part 2 - "The Inheritance", both the L&SWR and the LB&SCR electrification works were halted by the war. The SE&CR publicly stated before the war that they had no intention of going down the electrification route at that time. Five years after the armistice at the end of 1918, the world of railway electrification was very different. To start with an increase of over 25% in suburban traffic was recorded over the ten year period 1913 to 1923, and in addition the morning and evening rush hours were effectively more condensed following the general introduction of shorter working hours.

However, before any further work was authorised by the Board, the thorny issue of deciding the best electrification system for the future needed to be thrashed out. Walker set up a Departmental Committee under the chairmanship of E C Cox, the recently appointed Operating Superintendent. Cox had previously held a similar position with the SE&CR from 1911. The committee also included Alfred Raworth the New Works Engineer another SE&CR man whose background was originally in industry, followed by a spell with the L&SWR, before joining the SE&CR to plan their proposed electrification scheme. The committee took expert advice from a number of sources before recommending standardisation on the 600v DC system. The committee also recommended that the already advanced work on the extensions to the existing LB&SCR overhead system to Coulsdon North and Sutton should be completed as soon as possible, as a short term measure. Interestingly the committee does not appear to have looked at any alternative systems, i.e. 1500v DC overhead (much used on the continent), particularly as it was recommended as the future standard by the Kennedy committee in 1921 and by two subsequent committees.

Exactly where the decision to set up a committee to look at this issue originated from is not clear, but it was most likely at Board level, with the object of keeping Sir William Forbes and the rest of the Brighton contingent happy. It should also be noted that the LB&SCR Board had, in principle, approved further electrification to both Brighton and Eastbourne in 1918, and had authorised a resumption of work on its electrification scheme to Coulsdon (later Coulsdon North) early in 1922, and later to Sutton, both before the amalgamation. Could this have been an attempt at pre-empting a future Southern Board decision to abandon the overhead system soon after the Southern took office?

Over the years, many commentators have questioned the decision to perpetuate the L&SWR 600v DC electrification and abandon the apparently more advanced LB&SCR 6.7kv AC overhead system, which predated the DC by more than six years. However, was it such a controversial decision given the circumstances confronting the Southern board at the time? Remembering that following the end of the war it took just over five years to get the legislation for the amalgamation of the Railways through Parliament, on to the statute book and the new organisations in place. As mentioned above there had also been an increase of over 25% in commuting during the previous ten years. Is it any surprise then, that during the second half of 1924 and the early months of 1925, the press (just as bad then as today's multi me-

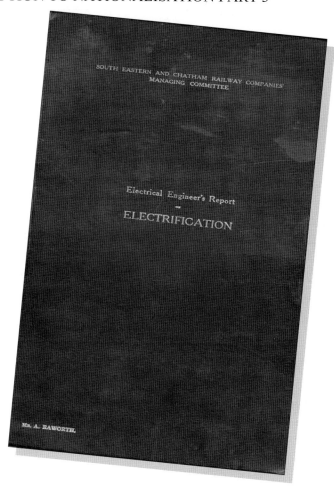

dia) were hyping up the many complaints being received of overcrowding and poor timekeeping, particularly on the steam-operated ex-SE&CR suburban services, which were often in rough riding six-wheel carriages, hauled by superannuated, life-extended, wheezy old tank engines.

The long-awaited electrification schemes promised by the three constituent companies after the war had yet to materialise, and the average traveller had little knowledge of the improvements the proposed electrification schemes would bring, let alone when. The old companies preferred to make their announcements as to proposed new works and progress on schemes in hand, at shareholders' meetings. This in turn had the undesirable effect of restricting the information available to the travelling public. Many old-style companies, and not just railway companies, were often less than forthcoming when it came to informing their passengers, customers and employees about their plans and expectations for the future. The L&SWR and later the Southern were amongst the better ones, judged by the standards of the day, the Southern in particular often using its house magazine as a vehicle for the purpose.

Clearly, from the management's point of view, the need was to get improvements on the ground in an effort to improve the company's standing with the public. Equally there was also a need to ensure that the company's interests were not compromised by adverse publicity. Michael R Bonavia gives by far the most comprehensive account of events on how this was achieved by the company, and in the process set up their future publicity

Top - *A down 8-car Waterloo to Guildford via Cobham service passing the former DECCA factory opposite Queens Road Battersea, formed of two 3 Sub sets with a 2 car trailer sandwiched between them. The leading set is one of the 1925 new build short underframe sets for the Guildford – Dorking electrification scheme. The fact that the train is travelling in the down direction on what is today's Up Slow indicates that the picture must have been taken before 17 May 1936 when the direction of running was changed on the centre pair of tracks between Waterloo and Durnsford Road with the introduction of the new flyover to take the Up Local line over the Up and Down Through lines on that date, it is also probably taken after the 1 December 1925 when the timetable changes came into effect (see text).*

Bottom - *One of the 1925 short underframe sets running in to Clapham Junction on the Down Local line with an Effingham Junction via Epsom service. The picture must have been taken after the photograph above, as what would then have been the Down Through line is now clearly signalled for up trains, having become the Up Local line following the commissioning of the new signalling and Durnsford Road flyover 17 May 1936, this picture can also be placed as having been taken before mid 1940 when Clapham Junction A Box, on the left of the picture received its 'Air Raid' protection roof. The signal box on the right hand side of the picture is the old LB & SCR signal box (there being no direct connection between the two systems at this point).*

machine, in his book 'The History of the Southern Railway', from which much of the following information is taken. Towards the end of 1924 considerable pressure was being exerted on the Southern Railway, by the press, to get on with the suburban electrification. The Board was clearly concerned about this; and how to counter it. Fortunately Walker was on good terms with the chairman of the Underground Group, Lord Ashfield, who was formerly Sir Albert Stanley, and, as President of the Board of Trade, was the nominated chairman of the Government's REC, Walker being the acting chairman throughout the war. On discussing the problems with Lord Ashfield It emerged that the Underground was also having trouble in returning operations to an acceptable standard after the war, but there appears to have been little mention of it in the press. The suggestion of Lord Ashfield was to recruit someone to the management team with specialist knowledge of the workings of the London press, to deal specifically with the Southern Railway's relationship with the papers.

Lord Ashfield went further, and put forward the name of J B Elliot for Walker's consideration; Elliot came from a family with a Fleet Street background and had already been appointed to the position of Assistant Editor on the London Evening Standard by the age of twenty-six but by the end of 1924 had decided to leave following a disagreement over policy. After an interview with Walker and discussions as to the exact nature of the duties expected, Walker offered Elliot a newly created position as 'Assistant to the General Manager for Public Relations'. Elliot accepted and took up his appointment on 16 January 1925 after which efforts to counter the press criticisms moved on swiftly. Walker addressed a meeting of local council dignitaries, aimed at heading off the growing criticism, with a detailed defence of the Southern Railway's position. No doubt the guest list was carefully chosen to ensure those that would able to take away good news would be invited. This was followed on the 22 January 1925 by the publication of an advertisement in all the principal London papers, setting out the Southern's position.

C F Dendy Marshall, records that the advertisement briefly set out what it had done during the war years (presumably by all the companies now formed into the Southern group) and the difficulties that the company now faced. At the AGM on the 27 February 1925 the chairman, General Baring, said that one of the reasons for the overcrowding was that hundreds of carriages had been withdrawn from service for conversion to electric traction. The charges of late running were countered by the chairman stating that of the 113,709 trains run each weekday 93% had arrived within five minutes of time (the figure of 113,709 trains run each weekday, quoted by Dendy Marshall, is clearly an error or misprint; it should have been per month. If this figure is divided by the number of weekdays in a typical month, taken as 22, Saturdays not counted, you get a answer for the total number of trains run of 5,168, which is more in line with the current figure of around 2,000 trains a day using Waterloo.), the chairman added that in 1923 the company carried 59 million more passengers, a 26% increase, over the 1913 returns (slightly more than figures quoted in other references). The new positive message was soon being conveyed to passengers and staff alike, the publicity carefully presented to gloss over the omissions.

Following on from the recommendations of the Departmental Committee report on which electrification system should be adopted by the Southern, the two existing schemes were proceeded with. The catch was that both ended up as reduced versions of the proposals previously announced by the LB&SCR and L&SWR. Both schemes were directly funded by the company.

Work to complete the LB&SCR overhead electrification to Coulsdon (Coulsdon North from 1 August 1923) and Sutton continued, but only the absolute minimum required to introduce electric trains was done, the proposed extensions to Brighton and Eastbourne being quietly forgotten. It has often been said that Walker was opposed to the decision to carry on with the work, but I doubt it, as he was an utter realist and would have been totally aware that the contractors would have to be paid for all the work already carried out on the scheme and for all equipment supplied and then ripped out having never been used. There would also have been a further wait of some years before a third rail scheme all the way from Victoria and/or London Bridge got as far as Coulsdon North and Sutton. Such a course of action was hardly likely to endear him to hard-pressed commuters, let alone the Board and shareholders. Additionally it would have been necessary to fund all the extra work, together with the abortive costs of such action; and given the expenditure committed elsewhere, any additional costs would have been most unwelcome. Originally it had been intended to introduce electric working to Coulsdon North and Sutton on 1 March 1925 but once again the electricity supply wasn't available in time and the opening was postponed until 1st April 1925.

New trains had been ordered by the LB&SCR for the services to Coulsdon North and Sutton, consisting of 60 driving trailer cars (40 thirds & 20 composites), 20 composite (2 types) trailer cars and 21 motor vans (universally known as 'Milk Vans') and in line with standard Brighton practice, all these vehicles were 'loose-coupled' as became common practice with later main line stock.. The fact that many of the vehicles were delivered in LB&SCR livery gives some indication as to just how far advanced this scheme actually was by the time the Southern took

over. 20 trains were made up from the new stock with two trailer cars either side of a motor van, usually with the driving trailer thirds outermost. As the trains were delivered from the builders, Metropolitan Carriage & Wagon Co. Ltd. of Birmingham, they were test-run on weekend services to Crystal Palace.

Concurrently the Southern was also proceeding with a truncated version of the South Western electrification scheme. Only the sections between Claygate and Guildford, Raynes Park and Dorking North via Epsom together with the Leatherhead - Effingham Junction link were now to be electrified: the electrification of the main line to Guildford via Woking being shelved. Work on the reduced scheme amounted to some 67 track miles and the provision of seven sub-stations, all fed from the existing power house at Durnsford Road Wimbledon, through lineside cables at 11kv, to the sub stations and then to the track at 600v DC. In some ways this was the first of the new order of electrification schemes, as it now included the provision of other incidental and associated works. The provision of a totally new station at Motspur Park was one of the first of many similar stations which consisted of an eight-car island platform reached via a footbridge from the adjoining roads, which in this case was very close to the existing level crossing on West Barnes Lane; and was built to serve the growing housing developments in the area. New bay platforms were provided at both Guildford (today's platform 1) and Dorking North (later altered to become the Down Loop platform 3), for terminating the new train service, without interfering with through services. Another new feature was the provision of a new carriage shed, servicing facility and train crew depot at Effingham Junction, all included as part of the scheme. This was constructed on what was previously waste ground on the down side at the country end of the station. At that time Effingham Junction was well out in the sticks, with only a few houses in close proximity to the station, and to accommodate the staff for the new depot the company built a considerable number of new houses in Old Lane, which was within easy walking distance of the station and new depot. As the existing signal box was sited at the junction end of the revised layout and only had a 20 lever frame it was replaced by a new modified L&SWR type 4 structure, placed about half-way between the depot entry points and the junction. The new box was equipped with a new 29 lever Westinghouse A2 lever frame and would appear to be the first application of what later became the standard Southern Railway mechanical lever frame. Assuming that Effingham Junction's A2 frame was the first of the new breed, it is interesting to note that a number of new Stevens style frames were being commissioned long after its introduction; giving rise to the question, was the new Effingham Junction frame in fact a prototype or just an off-the-shelf purchase to fit the revised remit and short timescales? It would certainly account for the unusually high number of spare levers (9) in the new frame.

The new services to Dorking North and Guildford were introduced from the 12 July 1925 (the same day as the first part of the Eastern section electrification was introduced), the formal opening having taken place three days previously, accompanied by considerable publicity. The new train service however, was not the immediate success that had been expected. Although the timetable was based on the successful and familiar principle of clock face departures, it had also been completely recast, with the added new feature of selective stopping patterns, which resulted in some services not calling at certain stations. The idea behind having a different pattern of stops for following trains is two-fold: it reduces overall journey time by not stopping at selected stations and can reduce overcrowding buy eliminating passengers travelling to and from some smaller stations on the more heavily loaded services. The new Guildford via Cobham services only stopped at Clapham Junction and Wimbledon before Surbiton and travelled via the slow lines, along with all the other electric services out of Waterloo. The Kingston roundabout service missed out Raynes Park as did the Kingston and Shepperton service which reduced the off-peak service at Raynes Park by six trains per hour, generating much complaint from those wishing to travel from Raynes Park to stations on the Kinston Loop and the Shepperton branch. The level of complaints resulted in the services being revised from 1 December 1925 (timetable changes came into effect much quicker on the Southern, 85 years ago!). The response was another complete change: Guildford via Cobham services were now routed over the through lines and ran non-stop to Surbiton, the only regular electric service to use of the through lines, apart from some empty stock workings, for the next ten years. All the other services were routed via the slow lines and most now stopped at all stations, a pattern of service that lasted well in to the 1960s.

Under the original SE&CR electrification proposals what became the Eastern section would have been electrified in three distinct stages; the first of these proposed to electrify what would today be called the inner suburban area. The proposal was to electrify services from: Victoria/Holborn Viaduct to Bickley and Orpington via Herne Hill and the Catford Loop, together with the Crystal Palace High Level and Greenwich Park branches; Charing Cross/Cannon Street to Dartford (by all three routes); Orpington, the Bromley North branch, the Mid-Kent line and the Hayes branch.

Like the revived pre-World War 1 (WW 1) L&SWR electrification, the Southern proposals for the electrification of the South Eastern section were a somewhat watered-down version of the first stage of the earlier SE&CR proposals of 1920. A new standard of 660v DC third rail electrification was introduced with the scheme and the work was to be carried out in two separate phases. Only the sections from: Victoria to Orpington via Herne Hill and Shortlands, Holborn Viaduct to Herne Hill, Loughborough Junction to Shortlands via Nunhead and the Nunhead to Crystal Palace High Level branch were included in the first phase. The implementation of the whole scheme was planned by the Southern from the outset and the decision to electrify the routes out of Victoria first, at the earliest opportunity, was clearly intended to counter continuing press criticism, and it made good sense, as it was relatively straightforward to deliver in the short timeframe proposed. To be able to carry out all the work that it had committed itself to, the Southern needed to establish a second third rail electrification team (the original L&SWR team was engaged on completing the Western section electrification), in order to achieve the rate of progress required and deliver the associated works on time.

Preliminary work on the first phase of the scheme got underway during the early months of 1924, with the demolition of Camberwell and Walworth Road Stations, both of which had short platforms and were by now disused, having closed early in the war, never to reopen. It was the costs of rebuilding stations like these that partly put paid to any ideas of the SE&CR electrifying the suburban area before WW 1. The tram system was to quickly cream off most of the remaining short distance traffic, removing the necessity to include them in the Southern's future electrification plans. Loughborough Junction and Brixton however, were extensively rebuilt for the new services. At Loughborough Junction a new 520ft. Island platform was built on the main line (Up & Down Holborn - the line to Herne Hill) and the platforms on the Catford Loop closed. There were also alterations to the junction track layout to provide for parallel moves. At the city end, complementary alterations were made to the track layout to enable all trains to access Holborn Viaduct Station. In the case of Brixton, again the platforms on the Catford Loop were closed (the site of the Up platform still being clearly visible today) and the main line platforms (Up & Down Chatham Main) were extended to 520ft at considerable expense, including extensive use of cantilever construction techniques and consequential bridge works. The problems at Herne Hill were somewhat different as the track layout dated from the early days, when many trains attached and divided at the station. Alterations to the track layout were made to ease speed restrictions through the station, together with a new island platform and an extension to the re-

King Arthur class No. E770 'Sir Prianius' on a down Holborn – Ramsgate via Herne Hill working (according to the headcode), passing through Sydenham Hill platforms before plunging into the depths of the 1 mile 381 yard Penge tunnel. No. 770 was new in June 1925 and judging from the superb finish of the loco it is likely that it has only just been delivered from the North British Locomotive Works in Glasgow. No. 770 also had the distinction of being the last King Arthur to be withdrawn on 24 November 1962. Also new were the conductor rails, the first public electric trains passing this way from 12 July 1925 on services from Victoria and Holborn to Orpington.

maining platform, to provide four 520ft. platform faces. Trap points were added to enable trains to approach the Up and Down loop line platforms from Herne Hill and Loughborough Junction respectively, at the same time as main line trains were using the through lines. Another new station, on a slightly different site, was built at Nunhead to replace the old one; again the new island platform design was used and was very similar to Loughborough Junction. Nunhead was opened on 2 May 1925 a little over two months before electric services were officially introduced on 12 July, making it the first of the Southern's very distinctive island platform stations.

Power for the newly electrified section was supplied by the London Electric Supply Corporation to the Southern Railway's new Electric Control Room and substation at Lewisham. In part 2, I covered the difficulties that the LB&SCR and the SE&CR had with obtaining power from the electricity supply companies and the continuity of the supply was also an issue, which had safety implications. The provision of its own control

room, in effect a switching centre, along with a direct supply in the form of seven supply cables delivering a three phase supply at 11kv 25 Hz (cycles) direct to the switching centre, gave the Southern a measure of security of supply that was previously only available by having their own power station, and generating their own electricity supply.

As electric trains were totally new on the Eastern section, as it was now known, the Crystal Palace High Level branch was used for crew training on the new trains from the beginning of April 1925, even before the new Nunhead station was brought into use (see above). On 8 June trial running began between St Paul's and Shortlands, using the new turn-back facility installed as part of the electrification works. The full electric service commenced on 12 July 1925, accompanied by the now usual fanfare of publicity, which was designed to deflect the continuing criticism of the apparent lack of progress on electrification. The new service ran well enough on the first day (a Sunday) but the first few days of normal service were less fortunate with the usual

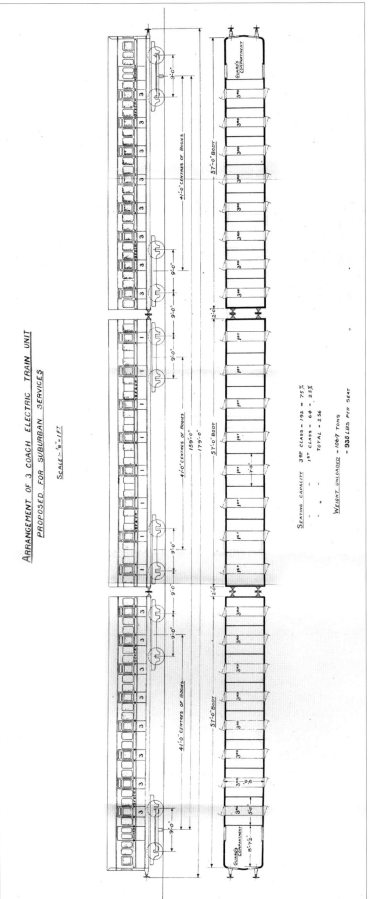

crop of blown shoe fuses, sticking brakes and two reported breakdowns in Penge Tunnel. The services to and from Victoria and Holborn Viaduct were arranged to maximise the number of pathways available for the regular steam-worked services, by timing the electric services a few minutes apart rather than the more usual even spacing, adopted elsewhere.

The second phase of this complex programme was to introduce electric services between: Charing Cross and Cannon Street to Orpington via both Lewisham and the direct line to Hither Green, joining the recently introduced services running from Victoria and Holborn Viaduct to Orpington at Chislehurst Junction; the Mid-Kent line services from Lewisham to Hayes, Addiscombe; the New Beckenham to Beckenham Junction spur and the Grove Park to Bromley North Branch. This was yet another example of a pressurised introduction; and can best be described as a quick fix due to continuing agitation by the press and the political lobby. This part of the scheme resulted in some extensive engineering and upgrading work, much of it continuing long after the introduction of the electric trains. To allow the introduction of electric working of services in the area, some observers describe the electrification of the lines around Metropolitan Junction and Cannon Street areas as temporary! The Southern even described it as such in official documentation. Even then temporary introduction could only be carried out after extensive engineering work had been carried out to strengthen the eastern half of Charing Cross Bridge (the company could only get limited parliamentary powers at the time) and to rearrange the running lines between Charing Cross and Cannon Street. The fact that they needed rearranging at all is down to the historical quirk of starting many services from Charing Cross and then running them round to Cannon Street and reforming the train before setting off for the country. The reverse procedure applied to trains arriving from the country, the whole rigmarole being carried out with much waste of time, and at considerable expense. The four running lines between Metropolitan Junction and the Waterloo end of Charing Cross bridge were originally laid out with the two Up lines on the outside of the two Down lines. These were rearranged to give the more conventional arrangement of two parallel Up and Down lines between these two points. As part of the work, the old overhead mechanical signal box at Charing Cross was demolished to make way for the new power signal box, which would control the new colour-light signalling system that was to form part of the next stage of the scheme. In the short term a temporary mechanical box was provided on the bridge deck. The temporary signalling arrangements created considerable work for the signalling teams, as at that time it was all mechanically signalled with Sykes Lock and Block working between the various signal boxes. On completion of the work the local lines were confined to the Eastern (old) section of the bridge, together with a couple of sidings, and served platforms 1 to 3. The single line directly leading to platform 4 was on a separate section of the bridge, and could be accessed via point work at the Waterloo end of the bridge. Both platforms 4 & 5 could be approached

General arrangement drawing for the proposed SE&CR three car electric sets.

this way and there was also a scissors crossover between platforms 4 & 5 to facilitate this move - alternatively they could be accessed from the through lines which were on the Western most section of the structure, which was the only access to and from platform 6. Apart from the subsequent removal of the sidings and the elimination of the scissors crossover between 4 & 5, together with the through lines' access to and from platform 4 at the Charring Cross end of the bridge, the layout provided on completion of the works has remained constant.

After completing the first part of their work on time and carrying out the temporary electrification works, arrangements were put in hand for a proposed introduction of electric working on 1December 1925. This was quickly postponed for three months as the necessary power supplies would not be available in time. Fortunately the section from Elmers End to Hayes was available from 21 September 1925 for staff training purposes. The new electric services to and from Charing Cross/Cannon Street were eventually introduced on 28 February 1926

Uniquely, the southern provided 55 brand new contractor-built 3-car units to cover the initial requirements for both the Waterloo to Guildford and Dorking North and the Victoria and Holborn Viaduct to Orpington services. However, the units for each section differed considerably, the most noticeable being the front end appearance. The 26 units for the Western Section looked rather like an updated version of the original L&SWR units, with their V-shape front ends. They were also unusual in that they were built on short underframes and, at 58ft 11ins over the headstocks, they were the only Southern electric sets to use this length of underframe. The motor coaches for these sets were built by the Metropolitan Carriage & Wagon Co. Ltd. and the trailer cars by the Midland Railway Carriage Co. Ltd. The control gear was supplied by Metropolitan Vickers (including the traction motors). The vehicles were formed into three car sets numbered 1285 – 1310, later renumbered 4301 – 4325. The other batch of 29 units destined for the Eastern section were very different in appearance with a much flatter front end which, with some refinements along the way became the standard until the end of the Southern's separate existence. These units also used what became the new standard length underframe of 61ft 11in (62ft.), used on all subsequent Southern electric suburban stock, these being the first sets built on the longer underframe. Again the motor coaches were built by the Metropolitan Carriage & Wagon Co. Ltd., but the trailer cars were constructed by the Birmingham Railway Wagon & Carriage Co. Ltd. The control gear was supplied by Metropolitan Vickers but with GEC traction motors, and they were initially numbered 1496 – 1524 and later became 4326 - 4354. One other feature that distinguished all the contractor-built sets was that intermediate coupling used between the vehicles within the set, was of the MCB automatic type, although this was later changed to the standard Southern centre buffer and rubbing plate.

Many reasons have been advanced as to why the Southern ordered new units for their first post-WW1 electrification schemes, rather than copy the L&SWR practice of converting some of the relatively new steam-hauled suburban stock for the purpose. From the management's point of view the company could not afford to get it wrong, and it is clear that they were under immense pressure not to make matters worse by withdrawing

extra carriages for conversion, particularly as the company had already publicly stated that one of the main reasons for the reported overcrowding was because many carriages had been withdrawn for conversion to electric working. Clearly the only option left open was to buy in an extra 165 carriages in the form of 55 new trains. This course of action had the added bonus of creating over one hundred and fifty additional carriages that could used to form part of a cushion while conversion work was carried out on the rolling stock required for the next stage of the electrification programme. Once new corridor stock started to arrive, it released some older compartment stock which could also be added to the pool of spare carriages. It is worth noting that the company had not yet reorganised Lancing Carriage Works and workshop space for carrying out the conversion work on existing stock was at a premium.

The next article in the series, "Part 4 - Continuing Investment" will look at the continuing electrification on the Eastern section, the conversion of the old Brighton overhead to third rail and the introduction of the first four-aspect colour light signalling in the world! The other important area which missed out this time was the rapidly moving events on the locomotive front and the introduction of the new standardised fleet of corridor stock.

My thanks to Alan Blackburn for providing a check on some of the more obscure details, Mike Christensen of the WWII Study Group and to Martin Stone for once again wading through the manuscript and pointing out the errors of my ways.

Assistant to the General Manager for Public Relations J B Elliott (later Sir John Elliott).

The railway navvy is by reputation, if nothing else, often tarnished as a hard living individual whose presence was more often tolerated rather than applauded.

Stories abound of drunkenness and rioting, many no doubt true, but less often reported were the sadder aspects of such an occupation, the time when accident, illness and the like could leave a man disabled, unable to continue his chosen life and so unable also to support a family let alone himself.

It was into this type of situation that the Railway Mission arrived. One convert from a navvy himself to a missionary was David Smith, and who maintained an album of the locations and incidents in which he was involved (including an amazing collection of construction views of the Meon Valley Railway: another plug for the new book!)

Amongst the David Smith album was this pair of images with the accompanying note. Clearly written to David Smith by another similarly engaged missionary (there is a signature to the original note but it is, regretfully, totally illegible), the portraits and story were no doubt intended as a morale boosting portrayal of the practical help that the mission could offer the working man.

The note is reproduced verbatim: complete with the odd perhaps questionable comment. Together with the other 450 odd images in the collection - other than those of the Meon Valley, few if any can be identified as relating to the south of England. Even so they present a remarkable glimpse at a group of working class men who are today often stereotyped, although clearly this depiction was not always 100% accurate.

Courtesy David Foster-Smith.

THE GOOD OLD DAYS?

"*This poor navvy - George Rickner, lost both arms and hands - by SER coppers while returning home from the Chislehurst Tunnel works on a foggy November night. There was no compensation by SER or contractor as he was walking on the wrong side (legally) although everybody did the same owing to the difficulty for pedestrians on the contractor's side. It occurred on a complicated network of crossings. In response to my appeal £12 was contributed by passengers, which moved the contractor to add £20 - without legal prejudice.*

"*The local N. M. Jery (N.M. = Navvy Missionary) kindly co-operated as Treasurer in raising about £50, sufficient to maintain wife and two children at 12/6d per week until his discharge from Guy's Hospital, also to purchase artificial arms and hands in the hope of a business livelihood. Work was kindly provided by contractors until completion of works when the most earnest efforts failed to obtain further employment for him. Rather reluctantly, as a last resort, I made a supplemental appeal to Ricker's own parish, Manston, Kent, to which he had removed and raised sufficient to purchase the organ, trolley and pony of picture.*

"*I selected the organ in the Italian quarter of London for £14 and the poor man now earns a comfortable, respectable livelihood by a weekly enlist in the localities where his case is known. It is found inexpedient to use his artificial limbs for this purpose beyond arm, arm, hook and bucket from his left shoulder because:*

1 . It would misrepresent his case to the public eye.

2. The picture of organ grinding would immediately destroy his costly limbs which he can use as expediously seen for writing.

"*He requires the help of his wife or nephew to grind the organ and is often accompanied in fine weather by his two little children on a box seat, as shewn in the picture.*

"*Altogether it has proved a very grateful and satisfactory case, as otherwise himself and family, most immediately have been pampered for life, having no kindred able to befriend them. I beg your acceptance of copy, as an instance of the practical aid of the Navvy Mission - often rendered to men who would otherwise sink under their trials. The poor family, who are most grateful, have just had this recent picture taken of themselves and have kindly provided me with half a dozen copies. Christmas 1906.*"

MORE ON PUSH - PULL WORKINGS

- see also SW11 and the front cover image of SW10

Gerry Bixley has kindly added some more details on the SR pneumatic air-control system as under. "The air control system was the 1909 LB&SCR which the SR adopted with the addition of vacuum braking for the carriages - in the case of the LB&SCR vehicles. Coaches adapted for push-pull and of LSW and SECR vintage, plus of course SR built carriages were already vacuum braked.

"The Westinghouse pump supplies air to the main reservoir to achieve 90 psi. From this reservoir air is supplied to an auxiliary reservoir through a reducing valve at 25 psi. One end of the regulator control cylinder (under the floor and linked to the regulator handle) is fed by the auxiliary reservoir at this reduced amount which keeps the regulator closed in normal circumstances.

"To open the regulator from the carriage driving end, the driver operates a lever which allows air from the main 90 psi reservoir to enter the opposite end of the regulator control cylinder. This pressure, greater than the 25 psi holding it 'off', pushes the linkage rod and opens the regulator. By reversing the position of the control lever, the high pressure air is exhausted and the auxiliary supply resumes its job of holding the regulator off or closed.

"There was an isolating cock in the loco can which closed off the air supply to the end which was not being driven whenever two push-pull sets were in use, one on either side of the engine."

ISLE OF WIGHT PUSH AND PULL

"As far as I know the IWCR Railmotor of 1906 was the Isle of Wight's first attempt at specialised 'economy' measures to deal with light traffic routes, if you disregard the use of Terriers in the way the LBSCR used them as motor train engines as an 'economy' measure. Perhaps the comparison of Island and mainland routes is not an entirely fair one to make, for the limitations imposed by the permanent way, underline, and loading gauges largely dictated the types of locos and stock available to the company managements. After five years service the loco and carriage portions were separated and the coach was equipped with a second bogie for use as an orthodox vehicle. Apparently there had been complaints ('Rails in the Isle of Wight' page 15 - A B MacLeod) of excessive oscillation in the coach. It survived as altered until 1949.

"The second push-pull vehicle was an adaption of an ex Midland 12-wheel clerestory composite by the addition of controls, small high up windows (presumably the driver had to stand up to see forward) to one end and the conversion of the compartment to a driver's compartment. At this stage it still retained the clerestory and 6-wheel bogies. IWCR No. 3, a small 0-4-2 tank provided the power. Purchased in 1907, the coach served as a push-pull vehicle on the Ventnor town branch. It is said that an ex LSWR vehicle was adapted to run with the Midland coach but

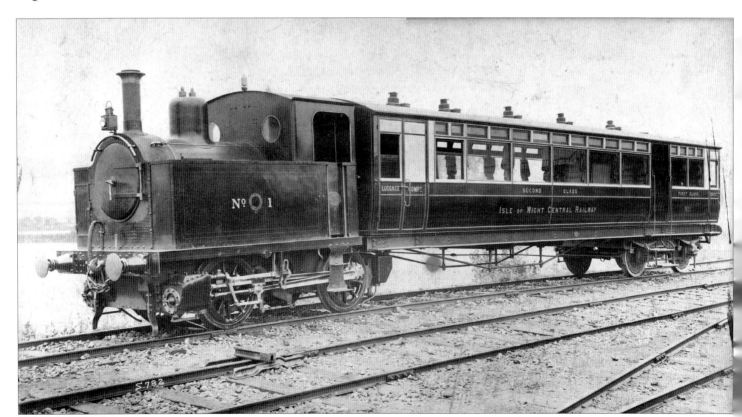

apparently no photographic evidence exists. The sale of the loco in 1918 caused the push-pull service to cease through lack of suitable motive power, and the coach returned to ordinary service. It was condemned in July 1937.

"According to 'Rails in the Isle of Wight' page 58, four ex SECR rail motor coaches converted to pairs of open bogie coaches were transferred for push and pull working but were returned in 1927 as not satisfactory for their duties. Other sources disagree and it is thought that the push and pull fittings were added on return to the mainland where duties in North Kent were taken up. For the record the coaches were SR sets Nos. 481: 6366 / 4110 and set 482: 6367 / 4109. The 63XX series denoted composites of course. The stay was a short one of two years and photos are again, very scarce of them in Island use.

"The next most likely push-pull units were sets Nos. 483 and 484 which were composed of LCDR 4-wheel coaches which had been sent over in August 1924. The brake Thirds were of slightly differing designs, 4111 of set 483 was 28ft long and 4112 of set 484 was 28ft 9in. I believe the longer vehicle had been a six wheeler. The composites, 6368/9 were 28ft long and had gangway connections to the brake Thirds. For some reason the gangways were at different ends of each composite. All these coaches ran as four wheelers. I believe they worked from Merstone with air control A1X locos but in 1936 set 484 worked the Bembridge line as push-pull whilst the turntable was enlarged to take the O2's. In June 1938 both sets were withdrawn and set 483 at least went back to the mainland where the underframes were used as service stock at Lancing Works.

"The reason for withdrawal of the LCD coaches was, perhaps, hastened by mainland electrification on the mid Sussex routes. By the mid 1930s some of the earlier LBSC push-pull bogie coaches had been withdrawn and scrapped as some LSW coaches were adapted for similar duties and electrification reduced the number of push-pull duties on the central section. The LBSC had been foremost in providing purpose built motor train stock, a fact not readily appreciated by railway enthusiasts, and some very good stock, less than 30 years old could be spared. The decision was taken to send three air controlled vehicles to the Island but two required some alteration. The vehicles selected were:—

Brake Third 3828 Built 1911 Set 731 IOW 4169 Set 503
Composite 6204 Built 1911 Set 731 IOW 6367 Set 503
Composite 6238 Built 1921 Set 715 IOW 6987 (Single Unit - also known as Set 503.

Set 731 was one of the first corridor push-pull sets designed for use on the heavily used Brighton and Worthing services. The two coaches were gangwayed and the corridor was merely an opening all the way along one side of the carriage, with no partition between it and the seating. The units comprised a guards / drivers compartment 14ft 2in long with sliding doors at the extreme end of the vehicle, five 5ft 5in third class compartments, a corridor partition, one more 5ft 5in Third and a 5ft 11¾in Third, wider presumably to allow extra circulating space at the gangway end. Seating was typically spartan LBSC and leg room was none too generous. A standard underframe with motor fitting pipes was used with two sets of double accumulator racks at the 'inner' end.

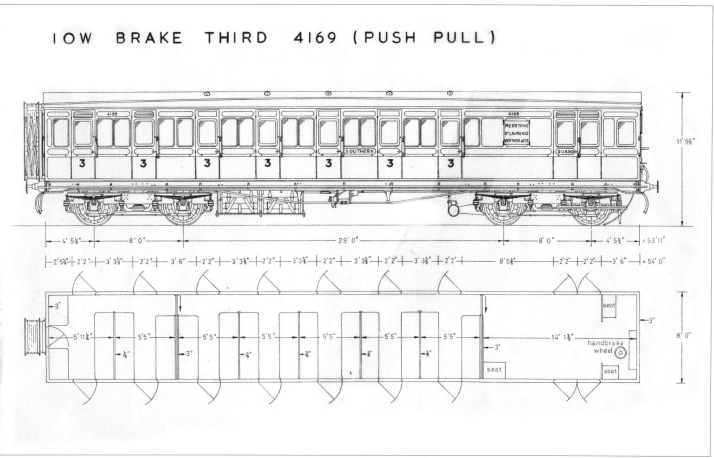

IOW BRAKE THIRD 4169 (PUSH PULL)

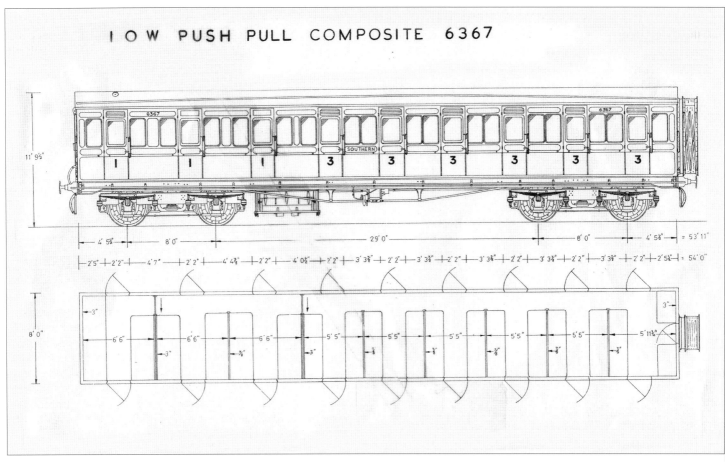

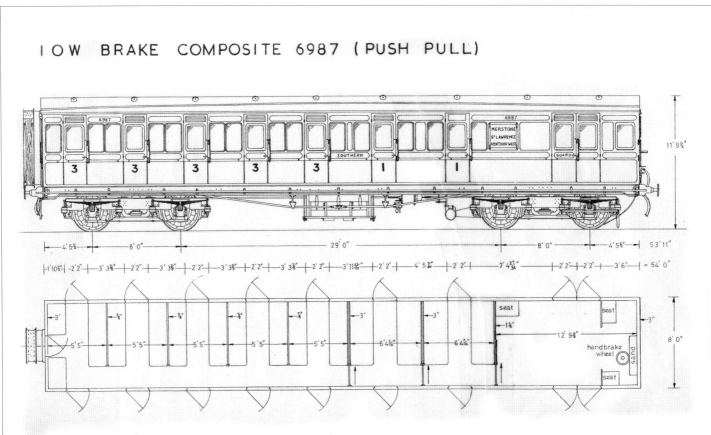

"The dynamo was unusually at the brake end. For Island use the sliding door was removed and the sides made good, and a set of double outward opening doors was substituted but centred 5ft 8in from the end of the vehicle. The driving end was altered from timber panelled to steel sheet but the original style was retained with four large windows, but electric sockets were fitted for the head/tail lamps. Drop lights were fitted in the sides adjacent to and opposite the driver's position. The original air brake system (altered to vacuum by the SR) was reinstated.

"The composite trailer was arranged (from the gangway end) onw 5ft 11¾in Third, five 5 x 5ft 5in Thirds, corridor partition, 2 x 6ft 6in Firsts, corridor partition, one 6ft 6in First. Originally electrically wired to the brake Third and having no accumulators, the trailer was fitted with single racks both sides at the first class end, but no dynamo. The boxes were of the same pattern as fitted to the various LBSC coaches by the SR having some LBSC and some SR characteristics. The WLS composite 6349 provides the observer a chance to see the only surviving boxes of the type fortunately. The Maunsell wheels were retained on both coaches. No. 6238 however was from a later period, and had formed part of set No. 715 which had been disbanded in 1938. Its companion had been the brake Third 3847 which ran as the last regular train on the Bluebell line just prior to its second closure. Originally a simple trailer composite with five Thirds and four Firsts it was converted as follows: - 12ft 9in van / driver's compartment, one 6ft 4½in First, partition, one 6ft 4½in First, partition, five x 5ft

5in Thirds, then gangway connection. Curiously the gangway was retained but locked out of use. Note that there was no extra circulating space at this end compared to the set. As with all LBSC side corridor push-pull coaches there were no large corridor windows, each compartment retaining its own doors and quarterlights as on ordinary stock, but the distance between the quarterlight on the adjoining thirds was as little as 2½in. The underframe was of a generally similar type to 6349 with large centrally placed accumulator racks each side. The brake end was similar to 4169. (No. 6349 is preserved on the Island.)

"Considerable discussion has taken place over the years as to whether all three coaches should have been classed as set 503. I have a SR diagram which shows the pipework arrangement indicating that the brake composite could be added at the other end of the train so that the engine was sandwiched if required. The same drawing indicated the single car could be used as such: were the three ever used together? If they were used together it would have been desirable to have the driving ends facing opposite directions of course.

"Oddly, on conversion to brake compo, No. 6987 retained all 18 torpedo vents which were fitted to the compartments. Photographs show both the set and the single brake compo working the Ventnor West line for which they had been intended but an unexpected problem arose when the O2s W35 and W36 commenced push-pull duties when it was found that their bunkers fouled 6987's gangway which was therefore removed and a sin-

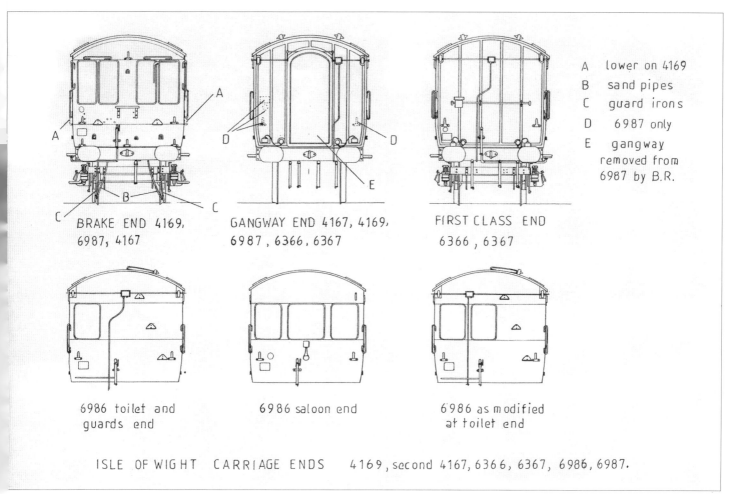

A   lower on 4169
B   sand pipes
C   guard irons
D   6987 only
E   gangway
      removed from
      6987 by B.R.

BRAKE END 4169,
6987, 4167

GANGWAY END 4167, 4169,
6987, 6366, 6367

FIRST CLASS END
6366, 6367

6986 toilet and
guards end

6986 saloon end

6986 as modified
at toilet end

ISLE OF WIGHT CARRIAGE ENDS   4169, second 4167, 6366, 6367, 6986, 6987.

gle panel substituted. At some time during the British Railways period No. 6987 worked on the Bembridge branch.

In 1947 a second push-pull set similar to 503 arrived for Bembridge duties on which it is believed it always ran loco hauled rather than push-pull. It was composed as follows: -

Type	No.	Built	Set	IOW No.	Set
Third	3825	1911	728	4167	505
Compo	6201	1911	728	6366	505

"The only distinguishing feature between the two sets was a minor difference in the van side and different accumulator boxes. For some reason during 1950 the set was split up but I believe it was later reformed and ran again to Bembridge.

The 1952/3 Island closures did away with all the normal duties (1952 Ventnor West and 1953 Bembridge) for all the push-pull coaches and all were withdrawn officially in December 1955 having been little used in their later days. They were all broken up at St. Helens Wharf. However, in typical Isle of Wight style, part of the brake van of No. 4169 was grounded on a farm and incorporated in some cattle sheds. "(This article by Gerry Bixley appeared in 'Wight report' 46, winter 1978/79.)

Gerry has also very kindly submitted more information, and plans, concerning the LSWR lorry featured in SW10. these will appear in SW14.

Issue No 14 of *THE SOUTHERN WAY* (ISBN 978-1-906419-53-0) should be available in April 2011 at £12.95

Contents will (we hope) include; Part 2 of the Middlebere Tramway: Part 2 of BR Mk 1 Coaching Stock on the Southern Region: Exeter Bank: The Southern Traveller: 11X tanks (and others) around Bognor: Memories of the Brighton Line, plus our usual Rolling Stock, Permanent Way, and Letters features.

To receive your copy the moment it is released, order in advance from your usual supplier, or direct from the publisher:

Kevin Robertson (Noodle Books) PO Box 279, Corhampton, SOUTHAMPTON, SO32 3ZX

Tel 01489 877880

www.noodlebooks.co.uk

editorial@thesouthernway.co.uk

The Last Word - Usually letters and comments received after a set date would, of necessity, be held over until a subsequent issue - as much to save moving everything around as anything else. This one, however, we just had to include. We are certain you will enjoy it as much as we did.

From David Brown of Orpington: "A few thoughts on Michael Harvey's interesting article. My memories of Redhill go back to about 1950 when various engine workings and shunting seemed to go on almost continuously during much of the day. Incoming trains from Reigate were frequently stopped at the Outer Home which was right opposite the tannery. The smell was memorable..... .

"The other story took place after the great train robbery on the West Coast main line. At the time Ron Love was a Traffic Inspector attached to Essex House and he reported to Jack Jennings, the District Movements Manager. Normally Ron was engaged in facilitating various signalling schemes, however, on this occasion, he was asked to spend time at Redhill to try and improve the working of mail traffic prior to Christmas.

"Apparently the normal process involved both railway and Post Office staff double handling every mailbag: e.g. Post Office staff would not move on to the trains, whereas railway staff would not move sacks on to or off barrows. This time Ron negotiated with the Post Office supervisor so that either set of staff would do both jobs.

"The effect was startling, in that timekeeping of trains improved dramatically. Even the London Bridge to Dover Night-Mail left on time. This was fine, except that the Post Office sorters due to travel on the service, and used to a later than scheduled departure, arrived just after the train had left.

"Big panic! The result was that the sorters were sent to Godstone, by Taxi, to catch up with their train and where the service had been specially stopped to allow the staff to catch up. The only problem was that the stationary mail train had been spotted by the local police, who, fearing a repeat of the great train robbery, had called in every police car for miles around.........". Happy days.